The Making of Americans

E. D. HIRSCH, JR.

The Making
of Americans

DEMOCRACY AND OUR SCHOOLS

Yale University Press
New Haven and London

Published with assistance
from the foundation established
in memory of William McKean Brown.

Designed by Sonia Shannon.
Set in Bulmer type by
Integrated Publishing Solutions,
Grand Rapids, Michigan.
Printed in the United States of America.

Library of Congress
Cataloging-in-Publication Data
Hirsch, E. D. (Eric Donald), 1928–
The making of Americans : democracy
and our schools / E. D. Hirsch, Jr.
    p.   cm.
Includes bibliographical references and index.
ISBN 978-0-300-15281-4 (cloth : alk. paper)
1. Public schools—United States. 2. Education—
Aims and objectives—United States. 3. Democracy
and education—United States. I. Title.
LA217.2.H57   2009
371.010973—dc22
2009011074

A catalogue record for this book is available
from the British Library.

This paper meets the requirements of ANSI/
NISO Z39.48-1992 (Permanence of Paper).

10 9 8 7 6 5 4 3 2 1

To the Memory of Albert Shanker

Contents

Preface

This book departs from and supplements my earlier books on education. It concerns itself, like them, with overcoming low literacy rates and narrowing the achievement gaps between demographic groups but places those themes within the broader context of the founding ideals of the American experiment, which have been a beacon to the world and ourselves. My goal in this book is to develop and explain neglected but fundamental principles that must guide our schools in our current historical situation if we are ever to achieve those inspiring ideals.

Our educational difficulties have arisen neither from incompetence nor from ill will but from adherence to ideas that have proved practically inadequate and scientifically incorrect. Although I reject the education world's antipathy to a specific, grade-by-grade subject-matter curriculum, I praise its emphasis on humane teaching methods. Accommodation of the two views is possible if partisan caricatures recede. But accommodation is not my main theme.

This book proposes a rethinking of American K-8 education from the ground up. It outlines what American public education must be if it is to achieve greater quality and equity, as well as sustain the brilliant founding principles of the United States. My focus is on the early grades, because acquiring a

core of commonality and civic commitment is most urgently
needed in those years to enable diversity and individuality, as
well as equal opportunity, to reign thereafter. The early grades
are critical for assuring later competence. A good *general* education in the early grades is the necessary foundation for citizenship, literacy, effective use of computers, and, in the new
economic era, for speedy and successful job retraining. Free-
trade agreements have been especially hard on American adults
because our schools have fallen behind in providing the adaptive skills and knowledge needed to adjust to new jobs. The
widespread notion that the early grades are places where students should learn merely basic skills of reading, writing, and
arithmetic rather than specific content is, we now know, a scientifically misguided concept that contradicts reality.[1] We have
paid a high price for a persistent adherence to this fallacious,
how-to conception of early schooling in which "critical thinking" is supposed to transcend "mere facts."

Ultimately, this book calls for a revolutionary change in
the concepts and policies that guide many reformers as well as
apologists of public education. If my arguments are accepted,
it will mean repudiating ideas and slogans that have dominated
early schooling for at least seventy years, and replacing them
with different and more fundamental ideas. I do not contemplate easy acceptance. Max Planck shrewdly observed that
professors do not change their minds: we have to wait for new
professors. But because we cannot afford to wait, I hope that
people outside the universities will enter the fray.

I begin by briefly describing the educational ideas of the
American founders and their immediate successors. Such an
excursion into history may strike some as an indulgence when

practical reforms are so urgently needed. But the best way to overturn an outworn tradition is to develop more adequate founding principles. Those currently followed in our schools are neither as intellectually novel nor as venerably American as their supporters claim. They came into force only in the 1930s. Some knowledge of educational history can help us escape its more recent fetters.

This book addresses the particularly American character of our education. While I argue that our schools need to replicate the technical successes of high-performing schools elsewhere, I stress that they have special aims also that arise from our country's transethnic character. Those characteristically American goals were identified by eloquent writers in the nineteenth century, nowhere more forcefully than by a young Abraham Lincoln in his 1838 speech "The Perpetuation of Our Political Institutions." American schools play a critical role in our attempt to accommodate different groups and ethnicities in a peaceful and harmonious unity without requiring them to abandon their private identities. America remains the most successful experiment so far in creating what the philosopher John Rawls called "a social union of social unions."

The elementary school has a special place in this great political experiment because it is the institution that prepares children to participate effectively in the common public sphere. Our ambition as a nation has been to give children from any and all origins a chance to participate there as equals, according to their "talents and virtues," as Jefferson put it, no matter who their parents are or what language or religion they practice in their homes. As Horace Mann, the great nineteenth-century propagandist for public education, foresaw, competence brings community. To equalize opportunity through schooling is to create competent and loyal citizens.

I dedicate this book to the memory of my late friend Albert Shanker, who was president of the American Federation of Teachers. I decided to write it while reading *Tough Liberal,* Richard Kahlenberg's fine new Shanker biography. Al's premature death a decade ago was a setback to American educational improvement. His unique combination of ideals, courage, and acumen was just what we needed—and still need—to reinstate the grand Enlightenment goals of the American school. His intellectual and political toughness and strong influence are irreplaceable. Al's intellectual biography is the very image of what American schooling was instituted to accomplish. When he started in the schools of New York City he did not speak English. No wonder he defended the great aim of assimilation at a time when it was unfashionable to do so. His adversaries liked to advert to the militancy of his earlier days as a union leader. But to those of us who knew the statesmanlike Al of the 1980s and 1990s, those early days were irrelevant. We were drawn to his unique ability to overcome the left-right polarization of educational issues. I was especially grateful to Al for championing my ideas when it took great courage to do so. I have been labeled a conservative, but Al saw clearly that I am not. He saw that it is essential to our future that the left and the right get together on American education. The need to get beyond facile liberal-conservative labeling is a recurring theme of this book.

1

The Inspiring Idea of
the Common School

In a picture in the Library of Congress entitled "The Common School," taken in 1893, you can just make out the face of the teacher, Miss Blanche Lamont of Hecla, Montana, wearing a sweet, ironic smile. For the photo she has perched some boys (and a dog) up on the support logs, and she has given a prominent place to the young boy in the front with the big hole in the knee of his pants.

Miss Lamont seems to be a person who might encourage vigorous recess and mix some fun into the rigorous tasks of the common school. These might have included exercises from the spelling books of Noah Webster, such as "What is a noun? A noun is the name of a person, place or thing," and edifying stories such as that of the gored ox. Other stories might have come from William H. McGuffey's *Eclectic Readers.* The multiplication table and other math facts and procedures might have been taken from the books of Warren Colburn. History lessons might have been based on Salma Hale's *History of the United States,* which, like other history books of the time, aimed "to exhibit in

Miss Blanche Lamont and the Common School of Hecla,
Montana, 1893. Courtesy Library of Congress

a strong light the principles of religious and political freedom which our forefathers professed . . . and to record the numerous examples of fortitude, courage, and patriotism which have rendered them illustrious." From other popular textbooks Miss Lamont would have taught the children art, music, penmanship, and health. All across the nation in 1893, whether in a quick-built gold-rush town like Hecla (now a ghost town) or in the multi-classroom schools of larger towns, American children were learning many of the same things. America had no official national curriculum, but it had the equivalent: a benign conspiracy among the writers of schoolbooks to ensure that all students would learn many of the same facts, myths, and values and so grow to be competent, loyal Americans.[1]

Since this country was founded it has been understood that teachers and schools were critical to the nation's future. In our own era, worried policy makers have fixed their eyes on our underperforming schools and devised new laws and free-market schemes to make our students more competent participants in the global economy. There is understandable anxiety that our students are not being as well trained in reading, math, and science as their European and Asian counterparts. Reformers argue that these technical problems can be solved, and they point to exceptional islands of excellence among our public schools even in the midst of urban poverty. But the worries of our earlier thinkers about education would not have been allayed by such examples and arguments. The reason that our eighteenth-century founders and their nineteenth-century successors believed schools were crucial to the American future was not only that the schools would make students *technically* competent. That aim was important, but their main worry was whether the Republic would survive at all.

It's hard for us to recapture that state of mind, but it is instructive to do so. The causes of our elders' concern have not suddenly disappeared with the emergence of American economic and military power. Our educational thinkers in the eighteenth and nineteenth centuries saw the schools as the central and main hope for the preservation of democratic ideals and the endurance of the nation as a republic. When Benjamin Franklin was leaving the Constitutional Convention of 1787, a lady asked him: "Well, Doctor, what have we got?" to which Franklin famously replied: "A Republic, madam, if you can keep it."

This anxious theme runs through the writings of all our earliest thinkers about American education. Thomas Jefferson,

John Adams, James Madison, and Franklin and their colleagues consistently alluded to the fact that republics have been among the least stable forms of government and were always collapsing from their internal antagonisms and self-seeking citizens. The most famous example was the republic of ancient Rome, which was taken over by the unscrupulous Caesars and destroyed by what the American founders called "factions."[2] These were seen to be the chief danger we faced. Franklin and Benjamin Rush from Pennsylvania, and Madison, Jefferson, and George Washington from Virginia and their colleagues thought that a mortal danger lay in our internal conflicts—Germans against English, state against state, region against region, local interests against national interests, party against party, personal ambition against personal ambition, religion against religion, poor against rich, uneducated against educated. If uncontrolled, these hostile factions would subvert the common good, breed demagogues, and finally turn the Republic into a military dictatorship, just as in ancient Rome.

To keep that from happening, we would need far more than checks and balances in the structure of the national government. We would also need a special new brand of citizens who, unlike the citizens of Rome and other failed republics, would subordinate their local interests to the common good. Unless we created this new and better kind of modern personality we would not be able to preserve the Republic. In *The Federalist No. 55,* Madison conceded the danger and the problem: "As there is a degree of depravity in mankind which requires a certain degree of circumspection and distrust: So there are other qualities in human nature, which justify a certain portion of esteem and confidence. Republican government presupposes the existence of these qualities in a higher degree than any other form."[3]

Our early thinkers about education thought the only way we could create such virtuous, civic-minded citizens was through common schooling. The school would be the institution that would transform future citizens into loyal Americans. It would teach common knowledge, virtues, ideals, language, and commitments. Benjamin Rush, a signer of the Declaration of Independence, wrote one of the most important early essays on American education, advocating a common elementary curriculum for all. The paramount aim of the schools, he wrote, was to create "republican machines."[4] George Washington bequeathed a portion of his estate to education in order "to sprd systemactic ideas through all parts of this rising Empire, thereby to do away local attachments and State prejudices."[5] Thomas Jefferson's plan for the common school aimed to secure not only the peace and safety of the Republic but also social fairness and the best leaders. He outlined a system of elementary schooling that required all children, rich and poor, to go to the same school so that they would get an equal chance regardless of who their parents happened to be. Such notions about the civic necessity of the common school animated American thinkers far into the nineteenth century. In 1852 Massachusetts became the first state to make the common school compulsory for all children, and other states followed suit throughout the later nineteenth century. The idea of the common school dated back much earlier in Massachusetts, and in 1812 New York State passed the Common School Act, providing the basis for a statewide system of public elementary schools.[6]

By the phrase "common school" our early educational thinkers meant several things. Elementary schools were to be universal and egalitarian. All children were to attend the same school, with rich and poor studying in the same classrooms. The schools were to be supported by taxes and to have a common, statewide system of administration. And the early grades were to have a common core curriculum that would foster patriotism, solidarity, and civic peace as well as enable effective commerce, law, and politics in the public sphere.[7] The aim was to assimilate not just the many immigrants then pouring into the nation but also native-born Americans who came from different regions and social strata into the common American idea. Abraham Lincoln, who was to ask in his most famous speech whether any nation conceived in liberty and dedicated to equality could long endure, made the necessity of republican education the theme of a wonderful early speech, "The Perpetuation of Our Political Institutions," given in 1838, long before he became president. The speech echoes Madison and Franklin in stressing the precariousness of our republic. In order to sustain the Union, Lincoln said, parents, pastors, and schools must diligently teach the common American creed.

It's illuminating to read the Lincolnesque speeches of the state education superintendents and governors of New York in the early and mid-nineteenth century. Like Madison and Lincoln, these New Yorkers understood that the American political experiment, which left everyone undisturbed in their private sphere, depended on a common public sphere that only the schools could create. New York State, with its diversity of immigrants and religious affiliations, was especially alert to the need to build up a shared domain where all these different groups could meet as equals on common ground. The speeches of the state's governors and state superintendents are filled with cautionary references to the South American republics, which were quickly collapsing into military dictatorships. Unless our schools created Americans, they warned, that would be our fate. As Governor Silas Wright said in his address to the legislature in 1845:

> On the careful cultivation in our schools, of the minds of the young, the entire success or the absolute failure of the great experiment of self government is wholly dependent; and unless that cultivation is increased, and made more effective than it has yet been, the conviction is solemnly impressed by the signs of the times, that the American Union, now the asylum of the oppressed and "the home of the free," will ere long share the melancholy fate of every former attempt of self government. That Union is and must be sustained by the moral and intellectual powers of the community, and every other power is wholly ineffectual. Physical force may generate hatred, fear and repulsion; but can never produce Union. The only salvation for the republic is to be sought for in our schools.[8]

As early as 1825, the New York legislature established a fund to secure common textbooks for all of the state's elementary schools, specifying that "the printing of large editions of such elementary works as the spelling book, an English dictionary, a grammar, a system of arithmetic, American history and biography, to be used in schools, and to be distributed gratuitously, or sold at cost." The aim, they said, was *not* to "make our children and youth either partisans in politics, or sectarians in religion; but to give them education, intelligence, sound principles, good moral habits, and a free and independent spirit; in short, to make them American free men [and women] and American citizens, and to qualify them to judge and choose for themselves in matters of politics, religion and government. . . . [By such means] education will nourish most and the peace and harmony of society be best preserved." Exactly the same sentiments animated the great writers of our earliest textbooks, including Noah Webster and William McGuffey. They aimed to achieve commonality of language and knowledge and a shared loyalty to the public good.[9]

Out of these sentiments emerged the idea of the American common school. The center of its emphasis was to be common knowledge, virtue, skill, and an allegiance to the larger community shared by all children no matter what their origin. Diverse localities could teach whatever local knowledge they deemed important, and accommodate themselves to the talents and interests of individual children; but every school was to be devoted to the larger community and the making of Americans. By the time Alexis de Tocqueville toured the United States in 1831 and wrote his great work, *Democracy in America,* this educational effort was bearing fruit. Tocqueville took special note of how much more loyal to the common good Americans were than his factious fellow Europeans.

It cannot be doubted that in the United States the education of the people powerfully contributes to the maintenance of the democratic republic. That will always be so, in my view, wherever education to enlighten the mind is not separated from that responsible for teaching morality. . . . In the United States the general thrust of education is directed toward political life; in Europe its main aim is to fit men for private life. . . . I concluded that both in America and in Europe men are liable to the same failings and exposed to the same evils as among ourselves. But upon examining the state of society more attentively, I speedily discovered that the Americans had made great and successful efforts to counteract these imperfections of human nature and to correct the natural defects of democracy.[10]

Today, every political poll indicates that most Americans believe the country is headed in the wrong direction—in many domains. Hoping to recover our roots, many have turned to the Founding Fathers and looked to them for guidance. Unexpectedly, I find myself doing so as well. It has taken me many years in the vineyard of educational reform to understand how American education lost its bearings. Some of this book is concerned with telling that larger story. A smaller part is concerned with my own twenty-five-year odyssey in the trenches of educational reform, during which I gradually came to recognize the true outlines of the story. To remain ignorant of that history is to remain trapped within it. What John Maynard Keynes said about economic policy applies equally to education: "Practical men who believe themselves to be quite exempt from any intellectual influence are usually the slaves of some defunct [theorist]."[11] We need to break out of the enveloping slogans that hold us in thrall.

The Public Sphere and the School

On PBS's *NewsHour with Jim Lehrer* a young Muslim woman in a headscarf, aged sixteen or so, was being interviewed. She was speaking earnestly about the Muslim community in the United States, and she was making a lot of sense. What most engaged my attention, however, and still grips my memory was her manner. This girl sounded just like my sixteen-year-old granddaughter. Her intonations were the same, and the smart, smiling, good-natured substance of what she was saying sounded just like dear Cleo—her vocabulary larded with "awesome" and "fantastic" and other enthusiastic expressions of the current youth argot. I thought: this girl is wearing a headscarf, but she is American to the core. I also thought about the ongoing controversy in France, where the government has barred Muslim girls from wearing headscarves to school. I do not doubt that this American girl wore her headscarf to her public school, and I would be surprised if anybody made a big deal about it. Friends have explained to me why France—another democracy, created a little later than ours in the eighteenth century—is now making such a fuss about Muslim girls wearing headscarves to school. I understand their explanations, but I think that France has failed to learn important principles from its own philosophers and our brilliant American Founders. Our schools and our society may not be doing as well as they should, but they are still doing some things right.

But how deep did this Muslim teenager's sense of solidarity with other Americans run? In a pinch, would she be more loyal to her religion and ethnic group than to her country? We always hope that none of us will ever have to make such a choice. In the United States we almost never have to, thanks to the political genius of America's Founders, together with the accident that they lived at the height of the Enlightenment, when principles of toleration and church-and-state separation were at the forefront of advanced thought. How deeply did she understand and admire those ideas? How well had she been taught the underlying civic theory of live and let live that, in human history, has proved to be the most successful political idea yet devised to enable people of different tribes to live together in safety and harmony? My guess, based on consistent reports of our students' lack of civic knowledge, is that she had not been taught very well.[12]

A lack of knowledge, both civic and general, is the most significant deficit in most American students' education. For the most part, these students are bright, idealistic, well meaning, and good-natured. Many are working harder in school than their siblings did a decade ago. Yet most of them lack basic information that high school and college teachers once took for granted. One strong indication that the complaints of teachers are well founded is the long-term trend of the reading ability of twelfth graders, as documented by the National Assessment of Educational Progress (NAEP), "The Nation's Report Card." The trend line is a gentle downward slope.[13] This decline in reading ability necessarily entails a decline in general knowledge, because by the twelfth grade, general knowledge is the main factor determining a student's level of reading comprehension.

This correlation between background knowledge and language comprehension is the technical point from which nearly all of my work in educational reform started. To understand a piece of writing (including that on the Internet and in job-retraining manuals), you already have to know something about its subject matter. The implications of that insight from my research on language shook me out of my comfortable life as a conference-going literary theorist and into the culture wars. My research had led me to understand that reading and writing require unspoken background knowledge, silently assumed. I realized that if we want students to read and write well, we cannot take a laissez-faire attitude to the content of early schooling. In order to make competent readers and writers who possess the knowledge needed for communication, we would have to specify much of that content. Moreover, because the assumed knowledge required for reading and writing tends to be long lasting and intergenerational, much of that content would have to be traditional.

The 1980s and early 1990s were not the best years to be saying this. At the height of the multicultural movement, which aimed to change and broaden American life, few educators wanted to hear that school should be more, not less, traditional in the content it imparted. My scheme to foster equality of opportunity was identified as right-wing, whereas anti-traditional school reforms that were labeled left-wing had the unintended consequence of depressing equality of educational opportunity—a paradox whose explanation will become clear in the course of this book, which will have justified its existence if it helps inoculate policy makers against premature ideological labeling. Left and right both need to adopt a nitty-gritty educational pragmatism that is based on science and the nature of reading and writing, and reach a broad, nonpartisan agreement about the democratic goals of schooling.

Fortunately, even in the late 1980s and early 1990s many educators accepted my argument that children need to be explicitly taught the knowledge silently assumed in reading and writing. Encouraged by parents and newfound friends in the education world, in 1986 I started the Core Knowledge Foundation. We created a model early curriculum, and in 1991 we began successful implementation in two public schools, one in suburban Florida led by principal Connie Jones, the other in the concrete wilderness of the South Bronx led by principal Jeff Litt. Both schools were enormously successful but—for reasons that I will explore later—largely ignored by educational experts (though not by the popular press).[14] Now there are more than a thousand Core Knowledge schools and preschools in forty-seven states.[15] The news about their practical success has spread by word of mouth despite intense opposition from educators and administrators.

To readers unfamiliar with my earlier books, the technical foundation for the larger educational and social issues discussed in this book will become clearer if I briefly retrace the scientific insights that resulted in the formation of the Core Knowledge schools. Back in the 1970s, when I was doing research on reading and writing, the field of psycholinguistics was just beginning to emphasize that the chief factor in the comprehension of language is relevant knowledge about the topic at hand. Those findings have since been replicated many times, in different ways and with varying constraints, both in the laboratory and in the classroom, and have held up robustly.[16] One early experiment used the following passage: "The procedure is actually quite simple. First you arrange the items in different groups. Of course one pile may be sufficient depending on how much else there is to do. If you have to go somewhere else due to lack of facilities, that is the next step; otherwise you are pretty well set." Subjects could not make sense of these sentences until they were given a title explaining the subject matter.[17] But you don't need an artificial example to make this point about the need of familiarity with a relevant "situation model" to understand language. Here's a naturally occurring example culled fresh from the online site of the British newspaper the *Guardian:*

> A trio of medium-pacers—two of them, Irfan Pathan, made man of the match for his five wickets. But this duo perished either side of lunch—the latter a little unfortunate to be adjudged leg-before—and with Andrew Symonds, too, being shown the dreaded finger off an inside edge, the inevitable beckoned, bar the pyrotechnics of Michael Clarke and the ninth wicket. Clarke clinically cut and drove to 10 fours in a 134-ball 81, before he stepped out to Kumble to present an easy stumping to Mahendra Singh Dhoni.[18]

Even if one knows a bit about cricket, this is at the dim edge of comprehensibility for most American readers.

Yet the words are familiar enough. Comprehension is not just a matter of knowing words. There is not a single word except maybe "leg-before" that I could not use effectively in a sentence. What makes the passage incomprehensible to me is my inability to construct what cognitive scientists call a "situation model." This is a highly generalized insight. It is hard to find an example where this premise does not hold. Comprehension depends on constructing a mental model that makes the elements fall into place and, equally important, enables the listener or reader to supply essential information that is not explicitly stated. In language use, there is always a great deal that is left unsaid and must be inferred. This means that communication depends on both sides, writer and reader, sharing a basis of *unspoken* knowledge. This large dimension of tacit knowledge is precisely what our students are *not* being adequately taught in our schools. Their knowledge deficit is the major reason their reading comprehension scores remain low.[19] Specific subject-matter knowledge over a broad range of domains is the key to language comprehension and to a broad ability to learn new things. It is the cornerstone of competence and adaptability in the modern world. A shortfall in conveying this enabling knowledge is a chief cause of our educational shortcomings—including our glaring failure to offer equal educational opportunity to all children.

In contemporary America, some fortunate youngsters are apprenticed to the knowledge assumptions of the standard American language from their earliest days because their educated parents and caregivers use that language at home. Other, disadvantaged youngsters are less familiar with the usage conventions and tacitly assumed knowledge of the standard language. Still others come from homes where parents are neither literate nor English-speaking. American schools need to help all of these students join the big-tented, all-accepting American public sphere by enabling them to become full members of the wider speech community with its tacitly assumed knowledge. An initiation into this public sphere does not require rejecting the private sphere that nurtured them.

Membership in this public sphere means mastery of the formal codes of speech and of the tacit knowledge that makes formal speech intelligible—shared information about football, civics, and so on. Some educators have wishfully asserted that our students will gain this shared knowledge through their pores by interacting with their peers and listening to tunes on iPods. The disastrously low and still declining performance on reading tests in the eighth and twelfth grades is decisive evidence that they do not gain this enabling knowledge, despite our schools' strong emphasis on reading under the No Child Left Behind act.[20] Indeed, the disappointing results of that law owe less to its defects than to flaws in the scientifically inadequate how-to theory of reading comprehension, on which so much time is being wasted in the schools to fulfill the law's provisions.

I am a political liberal, but once I recognized the relative inertness and stability of the shared background knowledge students need to master reading and writing, I was forced to become an educational conservative. The tacit, intergenerational knowledge required to understand the language of newspapers, lectures, the Internet, and books in the library is inherently traditional and slow to change. Logic compelled the conclusion that achieving the democratic goal of high universal literacy would require schools to practice a large measure of educational traditionalism. This insight has required a tolerance for paradox and complexity that, unfortunately, many have found impossible to accept. Their resistance has greatly slowed practical progress in American education.

The connection between liberal social ideals and conservative school practices was well grasped by the revolutionaries who founded American education.[21] In eighteenth-century America, early schoolbook writers like Noah Webster understood the need not only to set forth the grammar, spelling, and vocabulary of the American standard language but also to teach the tacit knowledge, shared by everyone in the public sphere, which was taken for granted in speech and writing. Hugh Blair also had this idea of shared background knowledge in view when he published his *Lectures on Rhetoric and Belles Lettres* in 1783—informing both Britons and Americans what they needed to know (besides the English Bible) to communicate in the public sphere. His book went though printing after printing in the United States: I find 124 different editions of Blair's *Rhetoric* listed in the catalog of the Harvard University library—surely one of publishing's greatest successes! Between 1802 and 1812 Noah Webster produced his *Elements of Useful Knowledge,* covering some of the highly varied topics he thought all Americans should know.[22] Beginning in 1836, William McGuffey produced another American best-seller in his grade-by-grade series of *Eclectic Readers.* He called them "eclectic" because, like Blair and Webster, he knew that effective communication and intellectual competence require shared knowledge over a wide range of topics.

More is at stake in updating this tradition of publicly shared knowledge than just enabling our students to make higher scores on reading tests. Those scores do correlate with a student's ability to learn and to earn a good living,[23] but they also connect with something less tangible: a sense of belonging to a wider community and a feeling of solidarity with other Americans. When we become full members of the American speech community, we belong to a wider group toward which we feel a sense of loyalty. In large human collectivities, shared language and the accompanying shared knowledge are the chief agents of the sense of belonging. When people speak of "ethnicity," their meaning always includes the idea of a language community. Too often, ethnicity is thought of as something deeper than publicly shared language and knowledge—something quasi-racial. But school-based Hispanic ethnicity, say, is no more natural or innate than school-based American ethnicity. Standard written and spoken Spanish, with its eighteenth-century dictionary and its school-promulgated knowledge assumptions, was just as artificially constructed as Standard American English, which was formed with the help of Dr. Johnson's dictionary and schoolmasters like Blair, Webster, and McGuffey.[24]

Since language itself depends on shared knowledge and values as well as shared conventions, the aim of bringing children into the public speech community is a more than linguistic aim. All children need to be taught the general knowledge that is silently assumed in that language community. Our schools need to assimilate into the public sphere not just new immigrants but *all* of our children, regardless of family background. That is a fundamental aim of schooling in a democracy and one that we are not serving very effectively today. "Assimilation" sounds like a political or ideological goal, but it is also very much a technical necessity for effective education, because reading, writing, speaking, listening, teaching, and learning require the possession of the shared tacit knowledge of the language community.

Horace Mann understood that shared knowledge is essential to our sense of solidarity and harmonious well-being. Often called the "father of American public education," Mann explained this concept memorably in his twelfth annual report to the citizens of Massachusetts, in 1848: "Property and labor in different classes are essentially antagonistic; but property and labor in the same class are essentially fraternal. . . . A fellow-feeling for one's class or caste is the common instinct of hearts not wholly sunk in selfish regards for person, or for family. The spread of education, by enlarging the cultivated class or caste, will open a wider area over which the social feelings will expand; and, if this education should be universal and complete, it would do more than all things else to obliterate factitious distinctions in society."[25]

How did we lose the insights of Blair, Webster, McGuffey, and Mann, so critical to the cohesive development of the United States? In the course of this book I will sketch out why we abandoned those founding conceptions and why more recent educational traditions, though well intended, have failed us.

My purpose is not to assert simply that the good done by Webster, McGuffey, and Mann was disastrously undone by the twentieth-century educators who overturned their principles. Though that is in fact the case, I will not hark back to a golden age that never existed. My aim is to rethink, from first principles, what our schools need to be doing now. We know more than any of our predecessors did about language and learning. We know more about the policies fostering high competence in the most successful national school systems elsewhere in the world. We know more about why our inner-city schools have been failing: not simply because of high poverty and family neglect but also because of content poverty and curricular incoherence. Compared to former eras, we have a far more capacious view of what makes up our multiethnic American identity. In sum, the new goals of our schooling do not depend on recapturing some idealized past. Such an aim would merely open an endless debate about the unfortunate way things *really* were during the WASPish days of Noah Webster and William McGuffey, whose schoolbooks served up significant doses of bigotry, pugnacious nationalism, and sectarian religiosity. The goals we need to set ourselves are those that promise a still better school tradition in the future.

The Community-Centered School

Although the specifics of schooling in the twenty-first century must be new, the larger aim upon which American schooling needs to be founded is the same as in Webster's day—to develop the common public sphere in order to liberate and safeguard the heterogeneous private sphere. In the United States I can form any private association I choose and worship as I please. The chauvinistic Webster thought such freedom made America superior to the Europeans: "America founds her empire upon the idea of universal toleration: She admits all religions into her bosom—She secures the sacred rights of every individual; and (astonishing absurdity to Europeans!) she sees a thousand discordant opinions live in the strictest harmony."[26] To accomplish this feat of harmony, Webster thought we would need to create a common public sphere by means of the schools. His dictionary and schoolbooks were elements of his tireless efforts to create this public sphere.

Not just Webster but *all* of our earliest educational thinkers argued that precisely because we were a big, diverse country of immigrants, our schools should offer many common topics to bring us together; if schools did so, they felt, we would be able to communicate with one another, act as a unified republic, and form bonds of loyalty and patriotism among our citizens. In 1795, the members of the American Philosophical Society announced an essay competition on the subject of the best system of education "adapted to the genius of the United States." The prize was divided between two outstanding contestants, Samuel Knox and Samuel Smith, both of whose essays advocated a national core curriculum and, in Knox's words, "a uniform system of national education." Knox's cowinner proposed a national board of education that would set up and monitor this core curriculum.[27] The significance of this incident is not just that these two educational theorists independently advocated the idea of a nationwide core of commonality in education but also that their views found enthusiastic acceptance by the members of the society.

This idea of commonality in the early curriculum was far from a radical idea in 1797, when the American Philosophical Society published the prize essays. It was already the consensus view of such earlier writers as Jefferson and Rush. Benjamin Rush, in his 1786 essay "Thoughts upon the Mode of Education Proper in a Republic," was quite explicit about commonality. He reasoned that the extraordinary diversity of our national origins argued powerfully for a core of uniformity in our schooling: "I conceive the education of our youth in this country to be peculiarly necessary in Pennsylvania while our citizens are composed of the natives of so many different kingdoms in Europe. Our schools of learning, by producing one general and uniform system of education, will render the mass of the people more homogeneous and thereby fit them more easily for uniform and peaceable government."[28]

The word "homogeneous" might horrify many who have been taught to honor individual differences. But these inaugural thinkers were not advocating what some might reflexively (and mistakenly) label "lock-step education." They were simply not focusing on the private dimension of schooling—the development of personal talent and individuality—an aim of *private* cultivation that they fully supported. Long before modern sociology they were focused on readying students for what sociologists now call the public sphere.[29] Many of their statements show that they were concerned with children's individual talents, and even with their private happiness, as well as their virtues. But their main emphasis was on the child's future public responsibilities as a citizen of the Republic.

Today, the idea of commonality is labeled un-American because it conflicts with our more capacious idea of American identity, which can no longer be described by the imperialistic metaphor of the melting pot but by the multicultural metaphor of the salad bowl. This is an oversimplification. Our early educational thinkers conceived of the United States as *both* a salad bowl and a melting pot—a federated union. Salad bowl and melting pot are not mutually exclusive concepts—and they cannot be if we are to have a bowl to hold the salad. The recent debates over multiculturalism have obscured the founding political conception of the United States, one of commonality with diversity, the *pluribus* within the *unum*.

Fundamental to this founding concept is the distinction between the public and private spheres of life.[30] The Founders expressed it with greatest clarity when speaking about religion, which I will discuss more fully in chapter 3, but this distinction was meant to apply very broadly in the American system. We operate in the public sphere whenever we vote, serve in the military, transact business, become a member of a jury or a defendant at the jury's mercy, write for a big, unseen audience, or encounter any situation where we wish to be understood by strangers. This public sphere is the melting pot, where common laws, a common language, and shared unspoken knowledge and values are needed to make the uttered language comprehensible.

The private sphere is a more capacious realm, especially in tolerant America with its protections against intrusive government and its freedoms of association, speech, and action. That is the sphere of the salad bowl. It is neither literally private nor purely individual; our diverse and ever-changing systems of association are, on the contrary, highly social. Political philosopher John Rawls has called us "a social union of social unions."[31] "Private" associations are private only in the sense of being out of the reach of government and enjoyed peacefully apart from our legal, civic, and moral duties as members of the wider public community. Philosopher Richard Rorty offered the "club" and the "bazaar" as an alternative image for the public-private distinction—a lot of private clubs facing out on a big, open public bazaar. Yet another image is very New England—private houses and churches surrounding a public commons, a space where all can consort as equals. For those of us who advocate the common school, this latter has the advantage of using the word "commons."

The conviction that our schools need to make Americans out of all children, native or immigrant, was a sentiment that grew in strength in the nineteenth-century common-school movement. This is not to suggest that state control of schools and commonality of content was ever complete. Localities were always reluctant to pay taxes or cede full control.[32] But the common-school movement succeeded in establishing the conscious goal of preparing Americans for the public sphere and was thus an authentic extension of the founding ideas of Jefferson, Rush, and Webster.

The basic structural idea is still sound. In the early grades of schooling in a democracy, the public sphere *should* take priority. No matter what special talents and interests we may encourage in a young child, all of us have to learn the same base-ten system of arithmetic; the same twenty-six-letter alphabet; the same grammar, spelling, and connotations of words; and the same basic facts about the wider community to which we belong. Most modern nations impose that kind of compulsory early education because neither a democracy nor a modern economy can function properly without loyal and competent citizens able to communicate with one another.

Under this founding conception, the early curriculum can be viewed as a set of concentric circles. At the core are the knowledge and skills all citizens should have. Beyond that is the knowledge, such as state history, that the individual state wants children to possess. Beyond that may be the knowledge and values agreed on by the locality. And finally, beyond that, are the activities and studies that fulfill the needs, talents, and interests of the individual student. From the standpoint of the public good, what must be imparted most clearly and explicitly are the central core elements common to all citizens of the Republic. These need to be set forth specifically, grade by grade, so that one grade can build cumulatively on the prior one, allowing school time to be used effectively and putting all students in a given grade-level classroom on an equal footing. This idea of commonality in early schooling is fundamental to the educational ideas of Jefferson, Washington, Rush, Knox, Smith, and Mann. The community-centered common school is a conception that needs to be updated and reintroduced.

The Retreat from Commonality

"The Retreat from Commonality" is the heading of part 3 of *Education in the United States,* by Robert Church and Michael Sedlak, covering the early twentieth century. In it the authors trace the decline of "the common school" and the common-school movement, now relegated in our educational histories to the eighteenth and nineteenth centuries. Why did this good idea fade?

There was nothing inevitable in the retreat from commonality. What happened was quite contingent. Shortly before the beginning of the twentieth century, with a ferocity fueled by nationalistic self-righteousness, advocates of a rival set of ideas attacked the common-school tradition—and even the idea of tradition itself. The new theorists said, "We are not like Europeans; we are not slaves of the past. We are a practical (and better) people who look to the future. Our methods of education must reflect that." Painting a bleak picture of the mindless rote learning of common-school education, the enthusiastic reformers heralded the advent of "the child-centered school."

The idea that began to take hold in the American educational community thus completely inverted the concentric circles I described above.[33] Instead of placing at the center of emphasis and concern the knowledge and skill that *all* citizens should possess, the new center was to be the individual child and his or her interests, talents, and needs. From concrete projects and activities, the child would build up skill and knowledge in a natural, motivated way. Even when social efficiency and vocational schooling were considered the principal aim, as they were by some of the new theorists, the focus would still be on the temperament of the individual student.

Above all, the traditional academic curriculum was to be rejected. Schooling would no longer be subject-centered but would instead be child-centered. Though a lot of ink was expended on such innovations as unbolting school seats from their orderly rows, the indispensable principle of the new approach was that specific subject matter was no longer to be determined in advance. Curriculum topics would emerge instead from concrete projects and from the interests of the child. Knowledge would be acquired naturally and indirectly. The child's "growth" would be constructed from within and be in accord with his or her temperament. Independent thinking would be encouraged, and passivity avoided.

The new conception quickly became dominant: it was promulgated with vigor in our teacher-training institutions by the 1920s and 1930s. From the outset, the movement employed black-and-white polarizations, asserting that it alone exhibited loving sympathy toward the child. It has held to a partisan refusal to acknowledge that a subject-centered common school might possibly be child-centered and loving in the *manner* of its teaching.

One consequence of the child-centered idea was to make controversy over the specific substance of the curriculum unnecessary. The choice of content would be secondary, even trivial: any reasonable material would fulfill the chief purpose of schooling, which would be to impart the generalized skills of reading, writing, figuring, and critical thinking. Even as I write this chapter, this conception is well represented in a recent edition of the *New York Times,* which contains numerous letters about education in response to a piece on the twenty-fifth anniversary of the famous 1983 report on American education, *A Nation at Risk.* The very first letter, from a teacher, ends: "High schools need to focus on critical thinking skills, not facts."

This succinctly summarizes the theory now taught in our schools of education—although *no* knowledgeable cognitive scientist agrees with it.[34] The how-to conception of schooling has been hugely attractive. It promised to solve technical and ideological difficulties at one blow without the need to mandate any controversial "top-down" curricular decisions. Today, it is just as powerfully ingrained in American education as the child-centered idea. Taken together, the child-centered idea and the how-to idea constitute the modern tradition of American education. Common to both is an antipathy to a set curriculum and "mere facts." Progressivism may have been the name the movement's proponents liked to use, but it could more accurately be called "the anti-curriculum movement." That is what I shall call it in this book.

The consequences of the anti-curriculum movement are apparent in the schoolbooks children are now compelled to use. A look at current language-arts textbooks reveals a stark contrast to Webster, McGuffey, and their descendants, not just in bulk and glitziness but in their lack of any guiding principles of shared knowledge.[35] As late as 1940, some common subject matter was still being consciously set forth in schoolbooks, but by the 1950s that was no longer true: commonality in the early grades had collapsed. After a long struggle, the new set of ideas had overmastered the earlier tradition of providing every child with shared knowledge and democratic values.

Not surprisingly, tacitly shared knowledge among Americans has waned. Moreover, the anti-curriculum, formal-skills approach has wasted enormous amounts of school time in endless, unproductive drills. The child-centered idea, which was intended to engage the child's interest, has led to an approach that, besides being unproductive, tends to bore children to distraction.[36] Cognitive science suggests that a content-indifferent approach to education *cannot* succeed;[37] and experience confirms that it has not. Starting in the 1960s, a decline in reading and writing skills of high school graduates began to be alarmingly apparent. Recently they have even declined somewhat further, despite the frantic emphasis on reading skills under No Child Left Behind. Scores on the verbal Scholastic Aptitude Test (SAT) declined from a peak in 1963 to a low point around 1990. Since then they have remained rather flat.

Some claim that this precipitous fall in SAT scores was due to an increase in the numbers of low-income students taking the SAT, but Christopher Jencks, who studies social policy at Harvard, has shown that the explanation is inadequate.[38] He observed that during the 1960s and 1970s, the state of Iowa, like every other, suffered a steep decline in verbal scores, yet Iowa was then 98 percent white and middle class. A sharp increase in the number of low-income test takers couldn't explain Iowa's decline in verbal skills. Looking at examples from textbooks, Jencks showed that the chief cause was what happened in the country's schools in the 1950s, when the twelfth graders were going through school. The cause of the decline was not so much an influx of low-income students but an influx of educators trained in child-centered, anti-curriculum ideas, along with an influx of skills-oriented textbooks reflecting the anti-curriculum point of view.

By the 1980s, many people were alarmed by the declining scores. In 1981 the secretary of education convened a commission to report on the state of American education; the report was issued in 1983. Titled *A Nation at Risk,* the report contained this memorable comment: "If an unfriendly foreign power had attempted to impose on America the mediocre educational performance that exists today, we might well have viewed it as an act of war. As it stands, we have allowed this to happen to ourselves."

The main practical outcome was an agreement by all the states to set up definite academic standards for their schools— the state-standards movement. But the policy makers had not foreseen that those in charge of creating those standards would be guided by the very same child-centered, anti-set-content tradition that had brought on the crisis. Even the vague word "standards" encouraged evasion of content. Those who had presided over curricular fragmentation were now charged with creating the new standards. The result often looked like this:

> Students will comprehend, evaluate, and respond to works of literature and other kinds of writing which reflect their own cultures and developing viewpoints,

as well as those of others. Students will demonstrate a willingness to use reading to continue to learn, to communicate, and to solve problems independently. Students will use prior knowledge to extend reading ability and comprehension. Use specific strategies such as making comparisons, predicting outcomes, drawing conclusions, identifying the main ideas, and understanding cause and effect to comprehend a variety of literary genres from diverse cultures and time periods.

Such empty guidelines (this one is from Arkansas) offer no guidance at all. The phrases could be copied and pasted into any grade level, and in fact that is how many states' language-arts guidelines are constructed. They are monuments to the continuing triumph of the anti-curriculum movement.

Fostering a core of commonality appeals to most Americans.[39] Polls say that when people on the street are asked whether it would be a good idea for the schools to build up knowledge cumulatively, with one year building systematically on the prior one, they generally say yes. And if they are asked, "Do you think a definite core curriculum is probably the only way schools can accomplish that goal?" the answer is a more reflective yes. "Would it be a good idea, considering the many low-income students who move from school to school, for there to be some commonality from one school to the next?" "Yes, definitely."[40] These common-sense ideas are so attractive to an unindoctrinated mind that one of the most pressing needs in American education is to understand why these practical goals—one might even call them necessities of good schooling—have been so difficult to institute. Why?

I have already suggested the chief reason; gradually in the twentieth century a new set of ideas began to guide our schools, causing them by the 1930s, to start losing their sense of urgent civic purpose. By the 1950s they no longer conceived their chief mission to create educated citizens who shared a sense of public commitment and community. Their main emphasis shifted to the individual student's personal development. It was as if the public school had decided to train students more for private than public life. This shift did not take place because teachers and schools had abandoned their sense of civic responsibility. Rather, twentieth-century Americans had become optimistic about America. They no longer worried that the very stability and peace of the Republic hinged on diffusing shared knowledge and preparing virtuous, loyal citizens who would subordinate private aims to the good of the whole. By the turn of the twentieth century, educators confidently believed that the public cohesion of the country was firm, and that schools should therefore concentrate on the growth and development of individual children by means of activities, without letting a lot of book learning get in the way. The needed knowledge would arise incidentally from immersion in concrete projects and "hands-on learning" rather than from deadly "rote memorization of mere facts."

In the 1930s, when the ideas began to take over, this new, anti-bookish method was said to exemplify the superiority of American openness to the future—though it originated in writers of the European Romantic movement of the eighteenth and nineteenth centuries: Jean-Jacques Rousseau, Johann Heinrich Pestalozzi, and Friedrich Froebel.[41] One distinguished American theologian of the 1930s, Reinhold Niebuhr, complained that educational thinkers of the early twentieth century, like other Americans of the time, exhibited a deficient sense of tragedy in their optimistic reliance on children's natural development.[42] Other early critics of the new educational ideas joined Niebuhr in criticizing an overly credulous faith in naturalistic and individualistic approaches to school learning. Overconfidence in the natural development of the individual, these critics argued, was at odds with effective schooling.[43]

We can now see that it was also at odds with the Founders' and Lincoln's sense of the fragility of the American experiment, whose perpetuation depends on the eternal vigilance of its schools and teachers. By the 1930s, the individualistic, anti-subject-matter ideas of child-centered schooling already dominated our teacher-training institutions, although some education professors did worry that the new emphasis on the individual child paid too little attention to the needs of society. One distinguished professor at Teachers College of Columbia University, George Counts, created a sensation in early 1932 at a meeting of the Progressive Education Association by telling his audience that if the new kind of child-centered education "is to fulfill its promise it must lose some of its easy optimism and prepare to deal more fundamentally, realistically, and positively with the American social situation." The movement, he went on to say,

> has focused attention squarely upon the child; it has recognized the fundamental importance of the interest of the learner; it has defended the thesis that activity lies at the root of all true education; it has conceived learning in terms of life situations and growth

of character; it has championed the rights of the child as a free personality. All of this is excellent; but in my judgment it is not enough. It constitutes too narrow a conception of the meaning of education. . . . The great weakness of Progressive Education lies in the fact that it has elaborated no theory of social welfare, unless it be that of anarchy or extreme individualism.[44]

Counts's hearers were so impressed that they immediately revamped the meeting agenda to discuss the social issues he raised. What happened thereafter is instructive. Educators began insisting that the fulfillment of the needs of the individual child *and* the fulfillment of the needs of society are inherently harmonious aims. All will be well, therefore, if the schools fulfill the needs of the individual child.[45] Today, our schools continue to yoke the two aims together in their mission statements—without altering child-centered pedagogy and an emphasis on individual differences.[46] In American public schools since the 1930s, child-centered wine has been poured into ever-new terminological bottles—the "open classroom" in the 1970s, "constructivism" and "critical thinking" in the 1980s, and "Individual Learning Plans" in the 1990s. Individualistic, anti-set-curriculum ideas still persist even in the face of the stern provisions of No Child Left Behind.

2

Sixty Years
without a Curriculum

In February 2008, the *New York Times* ran an article entitled "Dumb and Dumber: Are Americans Hostile to Knowledge?"

A popular video on YouTube shows Kellie Pickler, the adorable platinum blonde from "American Idol," appearing on the Fox game show "Are You Smarter Than a 5th Grader?" during celebrity week. Selected from a third-grade geography curriculum, the $25,000 question asked: "Budapest is the capital of what European country?"

Ms. Pickler threw up both hands and looked at the large blackboard perplexed. "I thought Europe was a country," she said. Playing it safe, she chose to copy the answer offered by one of the genuine fifth graders: Hungary. "Hungry?" she said, eyes widening in disbelief. "That's a country? I've heard of Turkey. But Hungry? I've never heard of it."[1]

Kellie Pickler presumably attended her local elementary school, so her geographical ignorance was probably not mainly her fault. It is plausible to lay most of the blame on the new ideas that started in a few model schools at the beginning of the twentieth century and gradually took over American elementary schools between 1930 and 1950, fully dominating them thereafter.[2]

The Anti-Curriculum Movement and the Long Slide

The new ideas and methods were presented as big improvements over educational practices of the past, and in some respects they were—especially in the very early progressive schools at the beginning of the twentieth century, when a newfound sympathy for childhood and the child's interests was put into the service of delivering a well-defined academic curriculum designed to produce good readers and writers and high-minded citizens. As the historian of education Diane Ravitch has pointed out, the new theories enjoyed a brief golden age at a handful of schools between 1898 and 1918.[3] It is hard to imagine better schools than those in the early part of the twentieth century: the old Lab School at the University of Chicago (est. 1896) or the old Lincoln School (est. 1917) at Teachers College of Columbia University. But the era of child-centered methods in the service of a definite curriculum and of community-centered goals was fated to decline. The strength of the progressive movement—its lasting contribution—was its empathy with childhood. Its fatal flaw was its faith that the knowledge Americans need would naturally develop when the child became fully engaged in concrete experiences without the encumbrance of a defined academic curriculum. In the partisan enthusiasm of the new dispensation, educational doctrines became black or white. A set curriculum became equated with harsh and inhumane teaching methods. The valid ideas of the new movement were thus grafted onto an anti-intellectual disparagement of "mere facts" and a repudiation of explicit, coherent approaches to the material that children needed to learn. Any compromise idea which proposed that definite, preordained subject matter could be imparted by *means* of the new child-centered teaching methods was not to be countenanced.

The lack of a specific, grade-by-grade subject-matter curriculum in most of today's public schools suggests that the most useful way of viewing the theories that transformed and badly weakened American public education is not by their self-description as "child-centered" but rather by their abandonment of a coherent academic curriculum. In actual practice, the movement's chief emphasis was less on the individual child, who often got lost in the fads of the day, than on abolishing traditional academic subjects. This anti-subject-matter emphasis was common to all forms and varieties of the new theories. Their fierce refusal to make an accommodation to definite subject matter now seems a tragic mistake, a kind of magical thinking that expects high academic achievement from students who have been deprived of a coherent academic curriculum.

Despite my many years in the reform trenches, I did not fully understand the centrality of the opposition to a set curriculum until a year or two ago, when I read a talk given by a brilliant opponent of the new movement, Isaac Kandel, in 1939. He said:

Rejecting . . . emphasis on formal subject matter, the
progressives began to worship at the altar of the child.
Children [they said] should be allowed to grow in ac-
cordance with their needs and interests. . . . Knowledge is valuable only as it is acquired in a real situation; the teacher must be present to provide the proper
environment for experiencing but must not intervene
except to guide and advise. There must, in fact, be
"nothing fixed in advance" and subjects must not be
"set-out-to-be-learned." . . . No reference was ever
made to the curriculum or its content. . . . The full
weight of the progressive attack is against subject
matter and the planned organization of a curriculum
in terms of subjects.[4]

Kandel is right. The most fruitful way to think about the ideas
that took over American elementary schools in the early twentieth century is to focus on this hostility to set subject matter.
It might seem odd to call the new child-centered theory an
anti-curriculum movement, since schools must offer *something* in the way of a curriculum. In that sense every school has
a curriculum, however fragmented or impoverished it might
be. But the general public believes with good reason that the
word *curriculum* implies predetermined subject matter in
history, science, language, and the arts. The chief American
educational movement of the twentieth century, the movement
that came to dominate our elementary schools, is an anti-
curriculum movement. This central historical fact explains
how it has happened that for more than half a century our public elementary schools have lacked a coherent curriculum, thus

denying children at their most teachable age a systematic introduction to the rich domains of human knowledge.[5] As Kandel perceived back in the 1930s, that is the nub of the matter. Kandel belonged to a small group of dissidents at Teachers College who called themselves "essentialists," thereby emphasizing their belief that certain subject-matter content was essential to an effective education in the United States. They formed a short-lived organization in opposition to the anti-curriculum movement. In response, leading progressivists launched what was to become a characteristic rhetorical response: the pro-curriculum professors were bad people, comparable (in the era of Mussolini and Hitler) to the "fascist menace." They were allied with such "enemies of progress" as "religious fundamentalists" and other "reactionaries."[6] A poignant story from the period is recounted by Diane Ravitch in *Left Back*, her gripping account of American educational history in the twentieth century. Michael Demiaskevich, a brilliant Russian émigré, wrote excellent books that showed the anti-curriculum movement to be inherently undemocratic in preserving social hierarchies and in offering a fertile field for tyranny and thought control.[7] Despite the books' distinction, the masters of the field denied him appropriate recommendations. He failed to gain the sort of academic job his distinguished work should have earned him. Isolated and in despair, Demiaskevich committed suicide.[8] Such determined protection of orthodoxy within the education world is now a problem for the nation, for there are now no longer real warring sects in American schools of education.[9]

Some of the reasons for this uniformity are accidents of history. Between 1910 and 1930, eighty-eight normal schools in the United States turned into teachers colleges, and these new departments required new faculty.[10] To fill the demand for personnel they looked principally to the mother of American teacher-training institutions, Teachers College, founded in 1889 and incorporated into Columbia University in 1898.[11] In the 1920s, hundreds of prospective teachers and prospective professors of education at Teachers College listened raptly to the lectures of the new theorists, including William Heard Kilpatrick, the author of the most influential pedagogical pamphlet in American educational history—"The Project Method" of 1918. (Projects are better than books and lectures.)[12]

The proliferation of education schools in the 1920s thus came at just the time when the new anti-curriculum theories dominated teaching at Teachers College, and thence came to dominate dozens of education schools across the nation. This was a fateful coincidence for the future of American education, for it determined that a single orientation of educational thought would thenceforth dominate in our education schools. The founders of the new college-level schools of education would train their successors in the new, exciting theories, and those professors in turn would train many more generations of teachers in true doctrine, down to the present day.

These new-minted teachers and administrators gradually carried the ideas into the public schools during the 1930s and 1940s. Here is Ravitch's description of the process by which the new ideas were imposed on schools across the country:

Curriculum revision typically began after an administrator attended a professional conference or took a course at a school of education, where he discovered that his school or district or state was out of step with modern thinking. He would return home and inform his teachers that they were going to work cooperatively to revise the curriculum, based on the latest findings of educational science. Professional consultants would lead the process. . . . In every district regardless of the nature of the community, regardless of whether it was rural, urban, or suburban, regardless of the local economy, the deliberations produced nearly identical conclusions. Although there may have been exceptions, there are no reports of curriculum revision in which teachers decided that the theorists were wrong. In the records of that era, there is no indication that any school districts went through the process of curriculum revision and then decided to make sure that there was a solid academic curriculum for all students.[13]

Thus, throughout the 1930s the new anti-curriculum ideas gradually prevailed in the nation's public schools. By the 1940s and 1950s the process was complete, and by the 1970s they had achieved perhaps their ultimate expression in the "open classroom." Here is a description of a third-grade open classroom in a New York City elementary school given by two proponents, Walter and Miriam Schneir, in a 1971 *New York Times Magazine* article:

What is most striking is that there are no desks for pupils or teachers. Instead, the room is arranged as a workshop. Carelessly draped over the seat, arm, and back of a big old easy chair are three children, each reading to himself. Several other children nearby sprawl comfortably on a covered mattress on the floor, a song they have written and copied into a song folio. One grouping of tables is a science area with . . . magnets, mirrors, a prism, magnifying glasses, a microscope. . . . Several other tables placed together and surrounded by chairs hold a great variety of math materials such as "geo blocks," combination locks, and Cuisenaire rods, rulers, and graph paper. . . . The teacher sits down at a small round table for a few minutes with two boys, and they work together on vocabulary with word cards. . . . Children move in and out of the classroom constantly.[14]

It took a lot of time for the teaching philosophy of an entire national school system to be displaced by a new set of ideas. Incoming teachers, trained in the new philosophy, had to replace older teachers and their ways. New schoolbooks gradually had to replace earlier ones throughout some fifteen thousand school districts. The child-centered, anti-set-curriculum transformation of our schools took place over a couple of decades from the 1930s to the 1950s.[15] If we take the year 1950 as the approximate date of the full, nationwide implementation of the new theories, we would expect their full impact to be visible in our high school graduates about twelve years later—around 1962. And in fact from 1963 to the mid-1980s there was a precipitous decline in the verbal and math SAT scores of twelfth graders.

As the graph makes clear, math scores have begun to re-

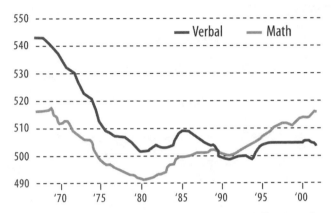

SAT verbal and math scores, 1965–2005. *Source: College Board;
AP.* Courtesy The Core Knowledge Foundation

cover, but verbal scores have not. The contrast between recent verbal and math scores is instructive. Under the pressure of public concern, our elementary schools have recently begun to adopt a defined curriculum in math. But not in language arts. Under the influence of the anti-curriculum movement, an American school finds it almost impossible to deliver a coherent, cumulative curriculum in that central subject.

The greatest squandering of school time in the early grades occurs in language arts, during the so-called literacy block—the two to three hours spent every day in pursuit of the ever-receding hope that trivial stories and mind-numbing drills will offer a shortcut around the need for the broad general knowledge required for progress in verbal ability. The long periods devoted to language arts are cognitive wastelands. Little coherent knowledge is conveyed during the freshest time of the day. The available language-arts textbooks actually discourage a coherent pattern of instruction. Here are some titles, listed in sequence, from the table of contents of the best-selling first-grade reading program by Houghton Mifflin: *A Dragon Gets By, Roly Poly, How Real Pigs Act, It's Easy to Be Polite, Mrs. Brown Went to Town, Rats on the Roof, Cats Can't Fly, Henry and Mudge and the Starry Night, Campfire Games,* and *Around the Pond.* These are stories our children might check out of the library and read for pleasure, on their own time. But making them the cornerstone of a language-arts curriculum in the earliest grades has exacted huge opportunity costs. Little wonder there was a big drop in verbal SAT scores.

I first became aware of a general pattern of educational decline in the United States some twenty years ago when I read a study put out in 1988 by the International Association for the Evaluation of Educational Achievement, the organization that compares school results from different countries. The study concerned the effectiveness of science education in seventeen countries and was a follow-up to a study undertaken some ten years earlier. The executive summary for the new study contained the following short sentence concerning what had happened to the scientific literacy of American fifteen-year-olds over the intervening decade: "The United States has dropped from seventh out of seventeen countries to third from the bottom."[16] From seventh to fifteenth in ten years! That was in 1988. Today, according to the most recent international study of science literacy in 2006, America has not recovered. In a study conducted by the OECD, an organization of developed nations, the United States ranks twenty-first out of thirty countries in the scientific literacy of fifteen-year-olds.[17]

Providential Thinking

Most of us think of *growth* and *development* in education as convenient metaphors for school progress, but in the anti-curriculum tradition they started out as something more literally conceived, as can be seen in the now-traditional phrase "developmentally appropriate practice." *Development* means unfolding; *appropriate* means suitable to the individual. The ideal of learning is thus an unfolding of the child's nature according to its own laws. Children, it was held, should "learn at their own pace." Similarly, the word *growth*, which filled the new theorists' writings, suggested that learning occurs naturally, as a flower develops from a seed. Educators began to speak of "reading readiness" as if readiness for reading were analogous to developmental readiness for walking and talking. Never mind that reading and writing did not arise from the nature of most people until well into the nineteenth century, when universal schooling came into being. Nor did place-value notation arise from the nature of *any* European until after the tenth century. The ancient Romans were not developmentally ready for modern math.

Today, educators are less attached to the vocabulary of natural growth. But even when they do not openly profess a faith that the child will naturally develop needed academic proficiencies, they still loyally promote the anti-curriculum principles that have been handed down to them, using scientific-sounding terms like "constructivism." "Research has shown," they say, that all real learning is *constructed* learning. This implies that the scientific way to educate is not to tell children dead facts but to place them in situations that will enable them to construct knowledge on their own. "Science says" that students should build knowledge through their own concrete activities. This is a relabeled, updated version of the "activity movement," under which academic gains were supposed to arise from using pots and pans and engaging in other concrete activities rather than from passive book learning. "Research shows" that such constructed knowledge is deeper and better than knowledge gained from lectures: "Constructivist teachers cheerfully accept that their most helpful role isn't one of direct telling and teaching. Indeed given the fundamentally internal nature of this deep learning teachers can't help by presenting rules, skills, or facts. Instead they create a rich environment in which the children can gradually construct their own understandings."[18] Despite the new terms, this claim is exactly the same as before—that academic learning will develop naturally and incidentally out of concrete activities better than from whole-class lectures and discussion based on an academic curriculum set in advance.

Mainstream cognitive scientists do not agree with these relabeled versions of progressivism. The term *constructivism* is a play on words, deployed to defend the faith that nonacademic activities will eventuate in academic "growth." This faith arises from faulty reasoning. Cognitive science has indeed shown that most knowledge is constructed. Ever since Frederic Bartlett's 1932 book on the constructed character of memory, cognitive scientists have known that understood meaning is something the mind actively constructs rather than passively receives.[19] But constructivism in this sense is quite general. If *all* knowledge is constructed, so is knowledge gained from a coherent academic curriculum. The scientific principle does not imply that children construct knowledge *best* out of concrete activities rather than out of verbal communications. And it turns out they do not. The most consequential flaw of the theory is that indirect, activity methods do not in fact produce sounder or deeper knowledge than a direct academic curriculum does. On the contrary, the results of constructivism are usually inferior. The activities favored by the anti-curriculum movement in the early grades turn out to be less effective in inducing knowledge and critical thinking than ordinary lively lectures along with systematic rehearsal and review.[20]

What then, in the face of the evidence, really underlies American educators' continued faith that the acquisition of unnatural skills like math and reading could arise naturally out of a child's activities? To someone like me, who happens to have a scholarly specialty in the intellectual history of Romanticism, this confidence in human nature is very familiar. These ideas arose in Europe and North America in the eighteenth century and flourished in the nineteenth and twentieth centuries in a wave of thought called the Romantic movement. But I will not overstress this historical provenance. The word *romantic* means different things to different people. It is best to focus on the basic principle underlying the belief that academic achievement arises best from a nonacademic curriculum.

That principle is providentialism.[21] The new theorists believed that the natural development of the child through concrete projects and activities would providentially lead to academic skill and social integration. *Providence,* from *pro-videre,* to see ahead, refers to God's ability to see the future and make sure that it works out according to his plan. In traditional religious faith we know that the future is beyond our control. However much we strive, we cannot completely know the future or what is ultimately for the best. Yet we have faith that a divine power has humanity's interests at heart and will ensure the ultimate good. Shakespeare said, "There is special providence in the fall of a sparrow." Providential faith is supposed to lead not to inactivity but to confidence and peace of mind. Providentialism is a highly appropriate mode of thought within traditional religion.

But when we introduce it into the secular sphere, doubts arise.[22] In the eighteenth century, influential thinkers who had abandoned literal belief in the tenets of sectarian religion shifted it to the secular sphere. They put their trust in a providential "nature." Toward the beginning of his autobiographical poem *The Prelude*, William Wordsworth captures the tone of this naturalized faith:

> The earth is all before me. With a heart
> Joyous, nor scared of its own liberty,
> I look about; and should the chosen guide
> Be nothing better than a wandering cloud,
> I cannot miss my way.[23]

Once faith in providence was brought down to earth, it was not a big step to place confident trust in the nature of the young schoolchild to lead to the right result. Education could not go wrong so long as artificial constraints such as math drills and desks in rows were removed. The anti-curriculum movement displaced providence from a transcendent God down into the developing nature of the child. That is exactly how the English critic and poet T. E. Hulme described Romanticism—a displacement of religious faith down into the secular sphere where it doesn't belong: "You don't believe in a God, so you begin to believe that man is a god. You don't believe in Heaven so you begin to believe in a heaven on earth. In other words, you get romanticism. The concepts that are right and proper in their own sphere are spread over, and so mess up, falsify and blur the clear outlines of human experience. It is like pouring a pot of treacle over the dinner table. Romanticism, then, and this is the best definition I can give of it, is 'spilt religion.'"[24] Hulme here identifies a basic difficulty with providential thought in education: religious trust is being placed in something secular that, as experience shows, does not warrant it. Such "spilt religion" is the source of the magical thinking that confidently expects academic learning to develop out of practical activities.

There is an implicit syllogism in the anti-curriculum movement: providential nature cannot go astray. As Wordsworth said, we cannot miss our way. We know that the activities-method of schooling is natural; ergo it must be the best possible one. Wordsworth also said, "Nature never did betray the heart that loved her."[25] But Wordsworth was wrong. Nature betrays all the time. The new educational theories handed over to nature those concrete, conscious choices of subject matter and skill that educators have an obligation to make as intelligently and worthily as they can, basing them on the needs of the community, on mainstream psychological science, and on a realistic assessment of human nature.

The Suppression of Dissent

This failed faith in natural development is sustained, unfortunately, by an intellectual monopoly within our teacher training institutions. I can illustrate this national problem with a personal anecdote. About twelve years ago I began teaching in the School of Education at the University of Virginia. It was the twilight of my university career. My teaching reputation at the university was pretty high. I had taught for many years in the College of Arts and Sciences, in the English department, where my courses on literary theory and the Romantic period continued to be oversubscribed and to get top ratings from students. I had arranged with the dean of the education school to teach a course on the causes and cure of the achievement gap between, on one hand, blacks and Hispanics, and, on the other, whites and Asians—a hot topic.

I expected to attract a lot of curious students and expose them to heterodox views in the literature. I had by then written two books on K-12 education. One of them, *Cultural Literacy* (1987), was a best seller, and the other, *The Schools We Need*, was placed by the *New York Times* on its rarified "Notable Books of the Year" list for 1996. Given the normal curiosity of students to take a course from the author of a best seller, I expected to draw quite a few students even though my work was critical of the dominant ideas in American education schools. I was surprised when I drew just a handful—ten or so students and no auditors. The next year the story was the same, as it was the year after that. In the third year, one of my students mentioned to me privately that I should be proud of the courage shown by my students; they were all in my class despite having been explicitly warned by members of the education faculty not to take the course.

I was astonished. This would not normally have happened over in Arts and Sciences, where professors, instead of shunning and shunting dissent, tended to exploit it. The controversialists would have held a big symposium and tried to create as many intellectual fireworks as possible. At the history department, even Thomas Jefferson, the university's revered founder, was the subject of various symposia in which anti-Jeffersonians were encouraged to have their say.

I am still stunned when I think about how students are being shielded from heterodox ideas in education schools, which are less like university departments than theological institutes where heresy is viewed as an evil that its members have a civic duty to suppress. The anti-curriculum movement's sense of righteousness, of being in possession of ethical rectitude and privileged truth, often has a religious flavor. Pro-curriculum heretics are to be seen as fallen souls who want to impose soul-deadening burdens on children and discourage lively, child-friendly teaching. Subject-matter-oriented people are by definition authoritarian, undemocratic, and right-wing. It is the duty of the education professor to protect prospective teachers from exposure to their ideas. Their writings must not be assigned, and if their ideas are mentioned, it must be in the controlled environment of a properly decontaminated textbook. This totalitarian feature of present-day education schools was demonstrated in a data-rich article by David Steiner and Susan Rozen analyzing the syllabi of education courses.[26]

Anyone interested in the schooling of our children should be aware of the ideological indoctrinations that our prospective teachers are currently required to undergo. The anti-curriculum doctrine is perpetuated by requiring prospective teachers to take a course in a subject called "Foundations of

Education." The textbooks available for this course uniformly attack the reactionary and inhumane tendencies of a content-oriented educational philosophy. The main categories used for describing the different educational philosophies are *progressivism, existentialism, behaviorism, essentialism,* and *perennialism.* These names (appearing with some variation in different textbooks) have their origins in terms such as "essentialism" that some of the intellectual movements originally gave to themselves.[27] But, as the textbooks helpfully explain, the theories all really boil down to this: "child-centered" (progressivism and existentialism) versus "teacher-centered" (behaviorism and essentialism). Child-centered theories are modern, forward-looking, and humane, while teacher-centered theories are old-fashioned, backward-looking, and inhumane.

I took an online test associated with one of these textbooks, *Teachers, Schools, and Society,* by Myra Sadker and David Sadker.[28] The test is called "What Philosophy Is This?" It gives a short description of a classroom scene, and you are asked to identify the educational philosophy that the classroom exemplifies. Here are a few examples:

> *Students are immersed in a world-cultures reading project, comparing animal stories and legends.*
>
> *Correct answer:* Progressivism
>
> *Older students are reading their stories to small groups of second graders.*
>
> *Correct answer:* Progressivism

Students are reading the history text, one paragraph per reader, up and down each row, and writing down the major names and events in each paragraph.

Correct answer: Essentialism

Students are reading their texts, and the best readers get their names put up on the bulletin board.

Correct answer: Behaviorism

Is it any wonder that idealistic prospective teachers would come to think that an academic curriculum with students regimented in rows and reading from "texts," not "stories," is inhumane as compared with the genial, child-friendly, and multicultural schooling of progressivism, where the reading is from "stories" and the desks are *not* lined up in rows? Currently teachers are being taught that progressivism is motivational and inculcates general skills, independent thought, love of learning, and critical thinking. By contrast, an academic curriculum is anti-motivational, requires rote learning of mere facts, and is antipathetic to independent-mindedness, love of learning, and critical thinking.

What's wrong with this picture? First, the classification of the different teaching philosophies is tendentious and arbitrary. There are many ways of describing educational philosophies, including, for example, the one I have been using here: pro-curriculum and anti-curriculum theories. Second, there is no inherent connection between establishing a definite curriculum and any particular form of instruction and classroom management. This is an absolutely critical point that is universally glossed over in teacher indoctrination. Why should an anti-curriculum approach be uniquely lively and humane and a coherent curriculum deadly and inhumane? Why should it be assumed that whole-class, teacher-driven discussions are dull and boring? A dishonest trick is being played on our prospective teachers. There is absolutely no reason why definite topics in world cultures and animal stories (described above as *progressivism* in the online quiz) cannot be part of a highly explicit multiyear academic curriculum and taught in all the lively ways described.

Perhaps the greatest barrier to dissent is the armory of effective, polarizing slogans that have been erected over the years, a propaganda effort that continues to preserve the anti-curriculum doctrine in the face of failure and decline. Ever since the 1930s, the identification of a set academic curriculum with an anti-liberal, reactionary, authoritarian, elitist, right-wing point of view has continued to be the most successful and persistent rhetorical maneuver of the anti-curriculum movement. It has won over many liberals and has influenced major philanthropies to oppose an elementary core curriculum—the feature most needed to carry out the truly liberal aim of greater educational opportunity.

Phrases such as "lock-step education," "rote memorization," "child-centered," "whole child," "social justice," and "critical thinking" have caused educational issues to be pitched in ham-handed ideological terms rather than in complex practical ones. For example, if you favor—as all cognitive scientists do—an explicit, analytical method of teaching children how to turn writing into the sounds of language—phonics—then you are called a conservative, whereas if you favor the naturalistic method of "whole language," you are a warm-hearted, child-centered liberal.[29] Once such polarized rhetoric is deployed, it is hard for teachers or policy makers to promote a pragmatic approach to schooling. As I shall show in the last chapter of this book, the fierce rhetoric of the education world continues to turn the heads of teachers and policy makers alike and to prevent bipartisan agreement on specifics of the elementary curriculum.

There *is* a grain of truth in educational rhetoric when it connects a set curriculum with a kind of conservatism. An effective core curriculum in the early grades—the chief practical need of American elementary education—must necessarily take a *somewhat* traditional flavor, if only because the foundations of mass literacy are very slow to change. There is little anyone can do to speed up this linguistic inertness, as I shall point out in chapter 4, "Linguistic America and the Public Sphere." Sociolinguists have shown that the widespread use of the written word has exercised a strong conservative influence on standard national languages and their correlative knowledge.[30] This does not mean that new, multicultural elements cannot also be part of the core for the early grades or that the received common knowledge cannot gradually change, but if we wish our children to understand the content of books in libraries and in daily newspapers, they will need to know who Winston Churchill was and what photosynthesis is. It is impossible to specify effective, literacy-enhancing content in the early grades without specifying traditional, commonly shared elements. Hence, an effective early curriculum is necessarily somewhat conservative in that it must conserve the traditional elements needed for public communication.

It is a facile act of sloganeering to object to branding such content as reactionary. Every topic included in a core curriculum must exclude some other topic. It is therefore all too easy to portray *any* curriculum that effectively enhances literacy as being right-wing simply by pointing out that it has failed to include particular topics. And even when those desired items are included, the content can and will be further challenged by the educational establishment for having omitted some other fill-in-the-blank item. The inherent vulnerability of *any* effective core curriculum to the charge of promoting a reactionary ideology is thus a powerful tool for preventing the development of *any* definite core curriculum at all. That is of course the aim— all too successfully achieved—of anti-curriculum rhetoric.

This conflict between ideology and effective educational reform thus raises an ethical issue for liberals and conservatives alike. Shall we have content-based early schooling that promotes universal competence and equal opportunity, or shall we have a nonspecific noncurriculum based on the providential, how-to theory of education that has not worked and cannot work? This issue seems to me tailor-made for a bipartisan effort by liberals and conservatives. Both should get together to scrutinize the anti-curriculum doctrines perpetuated by our schools of education.

Anti-Curriculum Thinking outside Education Schools

Yet liberal and conservative educational reformers have *also* tended to be resistant to the idea of a definite core curriculum. On that point there is unfortunate bipartisan agreement. Since the 1990s, the charter-school movement, led by conservative thinkers, has given parents the possibility of choosing alternatives to the low-performing public schools. Today about 1.2 million children are students in some 4,100 charter schools. Charter schools have been a very welcome innovation because they offer an early education that is not *necessarily* dominated by the anti-curriculum ideology. I am especially grateful to the charter-school movement for enabling several hundred Core Knowledge charter schools to come into existence.[31] But the movement as a whole has been inhospitable to the idea of a common core curriculum across schools, and many charter schools, like their regular-school counterparts, lack a definite or coherent curriculum. As a consequence, the performance of charter schools has been highly variable. If we decline to cherry-pick notable exceptions, the movement is a disappointment so far. Charter schools taken as a group have *not* performed much better than ordinary schools.[32]

Despite the discouraging data, proponents of school choice are sure that the theory is right. They believe that skeptics are not being patient enough. They argue that artificially induced barriers and start-up pains have prevented charter schools from conforming to free-market theory. But I have a different interpretation. I agree that the premises of free-market theory *are* applicable to schools. Experimentation, competition, incentives, and choice are productive forces in human affairs. Accountability is a good thing. Local administration that stays closer to the realities of an enterprise is usually more nimble and efficient than a centralized bureaucracy. All of that is true. The disappointments of the charter-school movement have been largely due to indiscriminate, technically ill-informed applications of free-market theory. Many of its premises about human action are sound if we take them as preliminary rules of thumb. But they need to be applied with deep knowledge of schools and of the multiple purposes of schooling in a democracy.

I once had an illuminating conversation with an intellectual leader of the charter-school movement—an economist. I complained that the manifestos of the program were all about theoretical structure, with little substantive discussion about the details of good schooling or about the implications of cognitive science and the wider civic aims of education. The approach, I said, seemed to be a meta-theory that simply asserted: if you provide choice, competition, accountability, and the right market conditions, you will ultimately get better schools. The details of actual schooling remained a black box. He smiled at me sympathetically. "But, Don, that's what economists *do*. They manipulate black boxes." This Olympian perspective is thought to be a virtue in that it avoids the well-known defects of detailed central planning. But it can also be viewed as intellectual laziness.

It may be true that if we are willing to wait long enough, and accept failure patiently enough while poor schools are weeded out, a hands-off approach may in the end produce good schools. But we cannot in good conscience sit on our hands, wait more decades, and sacrifice thousands of ill-educated children in order to let the theory work itself out. The very sort of objection that I raised earlier against the providential faith of the anti-curriculum movement can be raised against the black-box, free-market faith of the charter-school movement, as it has been widely applied. Effective school reform needs substantive knowledge about the best methods and aims of schooling. Few parents, exercising their free choice, have such knowledge. Many of them, in the absence of hard information and alternative voices, have bought into high-sounding anti-curriculum slogans. Many expect short-term gains, whereas cognitive science says that only a cumulative, multiyear approach can work. Despite parents' existential interest in the matter, they often know as little about what is needed for effective schooling as theoretical economists do.

Another fundamental question needs to be raised about the push for parental choice with charters and vouchers. Theorists of the choice movement seem to adopt the optimistic faith that when a lot of parents make individual choices for their children, that will also be good for the public weal. Structurally this optimism is similar to the providential faith of the progressives that a child-centered education will automatically be good for the community. Not necessarily. The public good needs to be considered in its own right. Charters and vouchers are paid for from the public purse. The charter movement needs to adopt a less individualistic approach. American schooling concerns not just the perceived goals of the individual parents for their children but also the goals of the larger local and national community that will make things better overall for everyone. We *all* have a stake in promoting an effective public sphere and more vibrant economy through our schools. The distinction between the private and public spheres is a founding conception that has made the United States a haven of freedom and an outstanding political success. But the public sphere cannot exist as a democratic vehicle for everyone unless everyone is schooled to participate in it. That goal requires a common core curriculum in the early grades. There is no practical way around that necessity.

When parents are asked if they think there should be a definite core curriculum in elementary schools, they generally say yes.[33] When the school-choice movement focuses sharply on expanding parents' options, it is concerned with the freedom to choose different schools, but it does not offer parents the possibility of a common, coherent curriculum. Because of the movement's lack of consensus about curriculum, charter schools must use the same fragmented textbooks as regular public schools and must draw on the same pool of teachers, who, through no fault of their own, have been offered inadequate subject-matter training by schools of education.[34] Charter schools cannot escape being part of this larger system. Building a marginally better car isn't very useful when the roads are full of potholes.

As a further practical point, there is nothing so far in the too individualistic approach to free-market school theory that would solve the problem of student mobility. Mobility rates— the percentages of students who move in and out of schools each year—range between 25 and 40 percent for suburban schools and between 45 and 80 percent for inner-city schools. More than 24 percent of all third graders have attended two schools since the first grade, and more than 70 percent of low-income students have attended two schools by third grade![35] A focus on parental choice and on the individual school glosses over the plight of those neediest students, who are forced to change schools in large numbers because their parents must move for economic reasons. This is again an illustration of the need for a more contextual approach in the charter-school movement, which is not exempt from the responsibilities of the public school system as a whole.

In short, existing charter schools would perform much better and competition between schools would be easier to judge if *all* American public schools of all types had to meet definite core curricular standards—openly arrived at—to build the public sphere. School choice works best in places like Ireland, where there is a common core curriculum in the early grades.[36] The individualistic, hands-off-the-curriculum approach, in contrast, has not worked in either regular schools or charters. This is not just because there are institutional barriers that are preventing the operation of free-market theory; it is because good free-market theory hasn't paid enough attention to the inherent constraints, goals, and substantive realities of the "industry" in which it operates. A school is a school. Charter or not, a good school needs a coherent, definite, grade-by-grade core curriculum.

Recently there have been some shining examples of changes in the thinking of those who support the charter-school movement, and they now stress the importance of a definite, coherent curriculum for some of the reasons I have outlined here.[37] But these remain exceptions. If all American public schools have civic responsibilities, so do American public charter schools. Continued opposition of charter-school theorists to a common core curriculum for all schools in the early grades means that the parental-choice movement has itself acquiesced in the anti-curriculum movement that caused our educational decline. If charters are to succeed, and if they are to contribute more significantly to the nation's well-being, that individualistic, anti-commonality prejudice will need to be overcome.

Education reformers on the left, opposed to charters, have just as fervently resisted making definite curricular decisions for early grades and have been just as complicit in perpetuating anti-curriculum dogma. Starting in the 1980s, an unfortunate alliance arose between the traditional anti-curriculum movement of education schools and the multicultural movement of the academic left. One reason that reading Richard Kahlenberg's excellent biography of union leader Albert Shanker impelled me to write this book was my realization that I, like Al, belong to the universalistic (and better) Old Left. The New Left has been particularistic, not universalistic. Its highest priority has been to secure recognition and status for women, blacks, Hispanics, and certain other groups.[38] Education professors eagerly joined New Left professors to promote the idea that *any* top-down imposition of *any* curriculum would be a right-wing plot designed to perpetuate the dominant white, male, bourgeois "power structure."

The chief terms of the New Left analysis have been "power" and "equality." Privileged knowledge of the past has to be replaced in order to reduce the power and status of dominant groups and increase the power and status of unjustly neglected groups. The New Left concluded that this goal implied replacing a traditional curriculum with a variety of curricula under which the schooling of black students would emphasize black achievements; Hispanic students, Hispanic achievements; female students, women's achievements; and so on. To see how far the group-identity idea has blocked specific decisions about curriculum, let's take another look at one of the state language-arts standards that I cited earlier: "Students will comprehend, evaluate, and respond to works of literature and other kinds of writing which reflect their own cultures and developing viewpoints, as well as those of others." This standard implicitly says: "Far be it from us to tell you students what you need to study and learn; you yourselves should provide the substance of the curriculum '*from your own cultures and developing viewpoints.*'" This neatly, if illogically, combines the education-school idea of individual development with the New Left idea of group identity. We are offered platitudes rather than concrete proposals, for one cannot reasonably insist that males will be compelled to study a female-centric curriculum or whites an Afro-centric curriculum. Make up your own. It is assumed that a diversity of identity-based curricula will providentially lead to greater social justice and higher educational achievement. This assumption of a pre-established harmony between group recognition and good educational outcomes makes no sense and has no basis in evidence. Shared knowledge alone enables communication and learning to occur in the public sphere. The educational failure of *all* anti-core-curriculum movements, left or right, may offer hope that the overarching goal of social justice might lure all parties away from anti-core-curriculum thinking.

In order to support its social justice aims, the left needs to promote rather than attack a common core curriculum in early grades. This is not a new idea. During the 1920s and 1930s a key insight of left-leaning *critics* of the anti-curriculum movement was their perception that the new "progressive" movement would lead to ever greater social injustice. Notable critics making this all-too-accurate prediction were the great Italian leftist thinker Antonio Gramsci and two left-leaning professors from Teachers College, William Bagley and Isaac Kandel.

The New Left has not quite known what to do with these thinkers. In the 1930s, leftists falsely characterized Bagley and Kandel as "reactionaries," but that could not so easily be said of Gramsci, who was imprisoned under Mussolini for revolutionary activities.[39] In his *Prison Notebooks,* he said that the new (anti-curriculum) movement is "advocated as being democratic, while in fact it is destined not merely to perpetuate social differences but to crystallise them in Chinese complexities." Gramsci defended instead "a single type of formative school" (the common school) for all students, precisely for the egalitarian reasons that the founders of American education favored such commonality. He explicitly stated that poor people must master the traditional tools of discourse and of learning if they want to create a "counter hegemony."[40] Gramsci was prescient: effective discourse depends on a mastery not only of the externals of language but also of the knowledge prerequisites that make effective communication possible. The New Left often invokes the philosophy of Jürgen Habermas but ignores the inconvenient implications of his plea for a common public sphere—just as it ignored Gramsci's not dissimilar conception for the "single type of formative school."

There are many things to criticize about the New Left—its lack of practicality, for example, and its elitist, jargon-ridden discourse. Especially suspect intellectually and ethically is the substitution of group identity for individual identity, though so many of us are hybrids, not pure blacks or Hispanics, or even pure male or female. We fall outside the current thought-net. Perhaps race and gender overkill was a temporary necessity to achieve higher social status for low-status groups. But the curricular views of the New Left have done little to promote the general welfare, raise the *economic* status of blacks and Hispanics, or provide the basis for effective job retraining in the information economy. To achieve that more fundamental form of social justice, the left will need to change its educational views. So long as it continues to advocate its anti-core-curriculum ideas, which militate against equal educational opportunity, it will ensure the continued need for affirmative action.

To the anti-core-curriculum extremists on both sides I say along with Mercutio "A plague o' both your houses." Surveys show that 80 percent of both teachers and ordinary citizens believe that a common core curriculum for early grades will greatly improve schooling.[41] Since the public instinct on this question is correct, extremist intellectuals on both the left and the right will serve us better if they change their minds on the matter of common curriculum—for the sake of higher achievement, equal educational opportunity, and solidarity.

3

Transethnic America
and the Civic Core

It is uncontroversial that schools in a democracy have a duty to
help form competent citizens. Who is against educating young
people so that they are able to judge the issues of the day, make
a good living, raise a family, and help keep civic peace and
order? But take the next step. We don't live in France or China.
It is a duty of American schools to educate competent *American* citizens—hence my theme: *The Making of Americans.* For
the past fifty years we have tiptoed around the idea that the
schools should form Americans. Child-centered theories of
education have focused more on individual formation than on
citizen-making. More recently, identity politics has emphasized membership in subgroups over participation in the larger
national community and has viewed traditional goals like assimilation and Americanization with suspicion, as an ideology
promoted by long-established WASP groups to continue their
domination. Disillusionment with the Vietnam and Iraq wars
caused many to view militaristic jingoism with distaste. In this
atmosphere, attempts to create guidelines for teaching Ameri-

can history in the schools have been occasions for fierce disputes between triumphal patriots on one side and critics of narrow nationalism on the other. Officials charged with creating state guidelines for teaching American history have often avoided the whole problem by producing abstractions that could apply just as well to the history of Zimbabwe:

Students use experiences, biographies, autobiographies or historical fiction to explain how individuals are affected by, can cope with, and can create change. Students will compare past and present similarities and differences in daily life. Students will examine how actions of groups and individuals cause change. Students will know that events can cause change and that change can cause events. Students will analyze how events can cause change and how change can cause events. Students will identify the dreams and ideals that people from various groups have sought, some of the problems they encountered, and the sources of their strength and determination.[1]

The strong patriotic sense of most Americans is not an accident but the fortunate residue of a time when the writers of American schoolbooks deliberately instilled common ideals and shared knowledge. But American nationalism at its truest is very different from the ordinary kind—unlike, say, the German nationalism based on tribal descent celebrated by Johann Gottlieb Fichte in the nineteenth century.[2] From the start, the idea of America implied the uniting of disparate parts into a single, self-invented federation that acknowledged a big distinction between the public sphere, which bound groups loyally together in this artificially created entity, and the private sphere, where freedom and autonomy were vigorously protected.[3]

If it is a duty of the schools to form competent and civic-minded Americans who can function in the public sphere, then we must confront the difficult issue of citizen-making with more forthrightness than in the recent past. I argued in the last chapter that we need to reorient the schools away from the child-centered approach—which has failed to produce either competent participants in the information economy *or* competent citizens—toward a more community-centered approach to schooling. To do so, we will need to clarify the "American" part of the school's responsibility. In order to reach agreement on a common core, we will have to rediscover some basic agreements about the United States and its ideals that are shared by both the left and the right.

Abraham Lincoln believed that the center of children's upbringing and schooling in the United States should be instruction in a *religious* devotion to democracy. Like the Founders from whom he took his inspiration, Lincoln was sensitive to the fragility of peace and harmony in a country where people of different religious faiths and ethnic origins bound themselves into one federation. His tragic sense of how precarious that unity is brought him very early to the view that parents and schools must diligently teach a common creed in order to sustain the union. His great Lyceum speech on that subject, "The Perpetuation of Our Political Institutions," dates to 1838—long before he became the central figure in preserving the unity of a nation riven by the issue of slavery. The urgency conveyed in this speech came not from the single issue of slavery but more broadly from his perception of the need to put solidarity, equality, freedom, and civic peace above all other principles—a public "political religion" that transcended all sectarian religions.

> Let reverence for the laws, be breathed by every American mother, to the lisping babe, that prattles on her lap—let it be taught in schools, in seminaries, and in colleges;—let it be written in Primmers, spelling books, and in Almanacs;—let it be preached from the pulpit, proclaimed in legislative halls, and enforced in courts of justice. And, in short, let it become the political religion of the nation; and let the old and the young, the rich and the poor, the grave and the gay, of all sexes and tongues, and colors and conditions, sacrifice unceasingly upon its altars.[4]

Lincoln conceived that America needed to be held together by a secular religion called "Democracy" that would be taught in our schools and would supersede all other religions. This religious conception was not a mere analogy or rhetorical flourish. With his accustomed profundity, he went directly from the writings of the Founders to the center of the American idea. Garry Wills has shown in his dazzling book *Lincoln at Gettysburg* how concisely Lincoln reformulated the American creed as an extension of the Declaration of Independence.[5] In his Lyceum speech, he did no less for the basic theory of American schooling.

Just six decades after the founding, Lincoln had a deep

grasp of the new political experiment on this continent, that it was intended to enable those who had been constrained in their thought and speech to become free and those who had been killing one another over points of doctrine to become safe. These two purposes were part of the basic political context of our founding and were central to the response of Enlightenment intellectuals to the recent religious wars and persecutions of the sixteenth and seventeenth centuries. Jefferson, Madison, and Franklin shared this Enlightenment revulsion against sectarian religion, especially the history of Catholics and Protestants murdering one another on theological principle. Following the lead of John Locke and other deistic prophets of toleration, the Deism of Franklin, Jefferson, Madison, and Lincoln renounced the cruel and bloody religious persecutions of the previous centuries. James Madison put it succinctly: "During almost fifteen centuries has the legal establishment of Christianity been on trial. What have been its fruits? More or less in all places, pride and indolence in the Clergy, ignorance and servility in the laity; in both, superstition, bigotry and persecution."[6] Even among those who did not officially call themselves Deists, skepticism toward sectarian theology had become widespread in the eighteenth century—even in such a representative and socially conformist personality as George Washington, whose tepid social Episcopalianism resembled the social Catholicism of Alexander Pope, whom he admired. Pope wrote: "For modes of faith let graceless zealots fight. / Theirs can't be wrong whose life is in the right."[7] In *Gulliver's Travels*, another work admired by the Founders, Pope's Protestant friend Jonathan Swift satirized religious antagonists as Big Enders and Little Enders who cruelly persecuted each other over the theological question of which end of an egg should be cracked open. In the 1770s, Goethe began *Faust* by having the hero say that he had, alas, studied theology ("und leider auch Theologie") and found himself none the wiser for it. For the intellectuals of the eighteenth and nineteenth centuries, the practical question—How shall we live with one another freely, kindly, and peaceably?— was more important than sectarian belief. Religious theory must not get in the way of freedom, civility, kindness, good humor, and, above all, getting along peaceably with one's neighbors. This was the central tenet of Deism accepted by most of the Founders, whether or not they openly embraced that new, rational religion of the Enlightenment.

Any debate about whether this or that Founder was or was not a Deist is made moot by the fact that Deism has no definite theology. Its major theme is that theology is trumped by ethics. Jefferson expressed this central tenet when he said: "It does me no injury for my neighbor to say there are twenty gods or no God. It neither picks my pocket nor breaks my leg."[8] His pocket and his leg were more important than his theology: the ethical and civic virtues that lead to public safety and the preservation of property are far more important than points of doctrine. As Leslie Stephen has pointed out, Deism is an *anti*-theological religion.[9] Our Founders expressly rejected "fanaticism" as a great political evil in the nation's new political religion. The idea that practical ethics and politics must trump theology or any other fanatical theory became *the* basic tenet of the United States—the source of our famous pragmatism and even of our anti-intellectualism. Freedom, justice, lawfulness, safety, and peaceful public order trump any tradition, doctrine, or scheme of thought that might get in their way. These are the founding tenets that Lincoln said we should teach in our schools.

Like the separation of powers in the government, the exclusion of belief systems from the public sphere and their inclusion in the private sphere was designed to pacify conflicts of power, beliefs, and interests. Opposed belief systems, rival ambitions, and group antagonisms, universal in human history, were to counterbalance one another through the constraints of law and language and, more positively, by a patriotism devoted to the good of the whole. In *The Federalist No. 10*, Madison famously argued that having a large republic where many factions contend with one another will make it more likely that "our zeal in cherishing the spirit and supporting the character" of the larger union will sustain civic peace and the common good.[10] He conceived that there would be a better chance for solidarity, peace, and harmony in having *more* rather than less diversity of religions and interests. Many subsequent political thinkers have picked up on Madison's idea. Here in America, "Heathen, Turk or Jew" would be encouraged to thrive along with Baptists, Methodists, Muslims, Congregationalists, Buddhists, Catholics, Episcopalians, and Pietists. The diversity of our factions would tend to encourage mutual accommodation and suppress fanaticism and would even have a moderating, ecumenical effect on the American versions of the religions themselves.[11] And what was true for religion—the most extreme and difficult case—could be made true for any other social grouping, economic interest, or system of ideas.

Abraham Lincoln understood that out of this brilliant,

practical arrangement there had arisen an American "heresy" so daunting that today it is discussed mainly in learned sociological treatises. If all the different religions, he implied in his Lyceum speech, are to be given free rein and tolerated in the private sphere to ensure the peace and harmony of the whole, then toleration is a higher idea than any secular religious tenet. Under this "political religion," the idea of America trumps any individual faction or sect. The peace and harmony of the whole is a higher thing than any of the factions that compose it. You can practice your religion as you please, so long as you help preserve peace and good order in the community and do not impose your belief on other persons and religions.

We are so used to this live-and-let-live idea that we scarcely notice that, on this principle, our constitutional commitment to America is more ultimate than any theological commitment to Catholicism, Judaism, or Islam. America is the meta-"church" that contains them all. Sociologists have observed that an emotional "civil religion" has grown up around this structure, enabling politicians to end speeches with phrases like "God Bless the United States of America." The God they are invoking here is a supra-sectarian God that encompasses "Heathen, Turk or Jew." The flag becomes as much a religious symbol as the Christian Cross or Islamic Crescent and indeed flies above them. The columnist Max Lerner once wittily remarked that "a country like America which in its early tradition had prohibited a state church, ends by getting a state church after all, although in a secular form." G. K. Chesterton called America the "only nation with the soul of a church."[12] The Pledge of Allegiance to the flag, composed in the 1890s, became a daily morning ritual in the public schools starting in the early twentieth century—a telling replacement for compulsory chapel. In the early nineteenth century, in their reports on the aims of the common school, the New York State superintendents eloquently expressed the Lincolnesque duty of the schools to teach the creedal dominance of America and its flag.

> As men we have the right to adopt religious creeds, and to attempt to influence others to adopt them; but as Americans, as legislators or officials dispensing privileges or immunities among American citizens, we have no right to know one religion from another. The persecuted and wandering Israelite comes here, and he finds no bar in our naturalization laws. The members of the Roman, Greek, or English church equally become citizens. Those adopting every hue of religious faith, every phase of heresy, take their place equally under the banner of the Republic and no ecclesiastical power can snatch even the least of these from under its glorious folds.[13]

What, specifically, does this imply for the elementary school curriculum? The most fundamental debate about the American political religion as it pertains to the duties of the school curriculum is whether America is primarily a formal structure that is sustained, as Lincoln implied, by core laws and a common language, yet open to constant changes of content, or whether America remains a system of Protestant, Anglo-Saxon values and traditions—a specific content *pretending* to be a merely formal structure. I first began to ponder this question in the 1980s when I read the brilliant essay "The

Priority of Democracy to Philosophy," by my friend and colleague Richard Rorty. His basic argument, congenial to the Founders, was that belief systems in philosophy or religion should be subordinate to "democracy," which does not itself need to be founded on any originating doctrine—not even the claim that we are endowed by our Creator with certain inalienable rights. That phrase was a rhetorically useful invocation in the Declaration of Independence, but liberty, equality, justice, toleration, and public order need not be grounded in any doctrines or values more ultimate than themselves. For the Founders, ethics and politics trumped theology, and they must also trump philosophy and any other personal, practical, or intellectual faction and special interest. This pragmatic, community-first approach to the ideals of liberty, equality, and justice opens up our politics to new content such as acceptance of homosexuality and racial equality. Our "political religion" is thus a formal structure of political and ethical principles rather than permanent specific content.[14]

This much-debated view is challenged by those who insist that the American polity cannot be detached from the Anglo-Protestant traditions out of which it originated. Liberals tend toward the more formal, open-to-change point of view and conservatives to the more substantive, stable, Anglo-Protestant side of the debate. Do we have any character at all? Or are we just a loose federation perhaps destined to fall apart, as Samuel P. Huntington suggests in his recent book *Who Are We?*[15] Some conservatives are made uncomfortable by recent acceptance of homosexuality and other giddy departures from our earlier traditions. On the other side, some liberals wish to banish a too-glorified mythic account of the American past from our early grades. Both sides *ought* to agree that the ideals that created the United States were glorious and that patriotic glorifications are very much to be encouraged in the early grades, so long as they retain a firm connection with truth. But some conservatives, including Huntington, seem to have a rather tribal, ethnic sense of what those ideals are. *Who Are We?* in its eagerness to equate American identity with the Anglo-Protestant tradition, makes only a passing mention of Deism, the Founders' actual faith.[16]

The ongoing argument between the open-ended formalists and the preservers of tradition is fascinating and subtle. Perhaps the most illuminating version of the debate took place between Michael Sandel and the late John Rawls, widely considered to be modern America's most important political philosopher. Rawls took the formalist point of view, Sandel the more substantive. It is telling, I think, that the debate between Rawls and Sandel became very technical and abstract—suggesting that in the end, the question may not have a clear right or wrong historical answer. My sympathies lie with Rawls and Enlightenment universalism. But there are powerful arguments on both sides, and since this issue remains disputed, our political religion, which demands consensus, cannot permit either side to take over the school curriculum any more than it could allow a sectarian religion to become the established church.

The core curriculum therefore must be consistent with what both parties to the debate can agree on, and this is, at a minimum, the more formal, structural account of our polity that emphasizes the abstract principles of liberty, equality, and toleration, as well as the uneven history of our efforts to make them prevail. This was the consensus approach of the curriculum makers in the nineteenth and early twentieth centuries, who aimed "to exhibit in a strong light the principles of religious and political freedom which our forefathers professed . . . and to record the numerous examples of fortitude, courage, and patriotism which have rendered them illustrious."[17] This basic aim must no doubt be continually adjusted. The cast of historical characters now will be more inclusive than in the past. Decisions about common content in the early school curriculum need to accommodate both liberal and conservative views about American traditions. It seems to me that both sides stress a shared duty to liberty, equality, justice, and civic order and to the general welfare of the wider national community, which argues for a primary emphasis on these abstract principles. Local communities can, if they wish, include further traditions and values.

Both sides of the debate can also agree that we need a more content-rich public sphere than we currently have. The early school curriculum needs to offer enough substantial commonality of content to connect each American with the larger community of citizens. Students need to leave school with a good understanding of the civic principles under which the United States operates and with an emotional commitment to making this political experiment continue to work. They need to possess the specific, concrete knowledge that will enable them to communicate with one another in the standard language across time and space. That much substantial content is required for our civic life to function. (The specifics of what this consensus core might look like are set out in appendix 1.)

If we manage to sustain and nourish the American public

sphere by means of the schools, then we will not need to worry, as Huntington does, about our private spheres diverging in unpredictable multilingual, multiethnic directions. Individuals and communities may diverge as they please, and the inspiring civic and linguistic core promulgated by our schools will be able to sustain us. The consensus common core, no longer preoccupied with imposing a particularist tribal American identity, will take pleasure in the exuberance and endless diversity of the American private sphere. A notable statement of this antiparticularist sentiment is found in Herman Melville's novel *Redburn* (1849):

> There is something in the contemplation of the mode in which America has been settled, that, in a noble breast, should forever extinguish the prejudices of national dislikes. Settled by the people of all nations, all nations may claim her for their own. You can not spill a drop of American blood without spilling the blood of the whole world. Be he Englishman, Frenchman, German, Dane, or Scot; the European who scoffs at an American, calls his own brother Raca, and stands in danger of the judgment. We are not a narrow tribe of men, with a bigoted Hebrew nationality—whose blood has been debased in the attempt to ennoble it, by maintaining an exclusive succession among ourselves. No: our blood is as the flood of the Amazon, made up of a thousand noble currents all pouring into one. We are not a nation, so much as a world; for unless we may claim all the world for our sire, like Melchisedec, we are without father or mother. For who was

our father and our mother? Or can we point to any Ro-
mulus and Remus for our founders? Our ancestry is
lost in the universal paternity; and Caesar and Alfred,
St. Paul and Luther, and Homer and Shakespeare are
as much ours as Washington, who is as much the
world's as our own. We are the heirs of all time, and
with all nations we divide our inheritance. On this
Western Hemisphere all tribes and people are forming
into one federated whole; and there is a future which
shall see the estranged children of Adam restored as to
the old hearthstone in Eden. The other world beyond
this, which was longed for by the devout before Columbus' time, was found in the New; and the deep-sea-
lead, that first struck these soundings, brought up the
soil of Earth's Paradise. Not a Paradise then, or now;
but to be made so, at God's good pleasure, and in the
fullness and mellowness of time. The seed is sown, and
the harvest must come; and our children's children, on
the world's jubilee morning, shall all go with their sick-
les to the reaping. Then shall the curse of Babel be re-
voked, a new Pentecost come, and the language they
shall speak shall be the language of Britain.[18]

   This thrilling passage is the imaginative, Romantic, plural-
ist aspect of the Enlightenment cosmopolitanism that founded
us. "On this Western Hemisphere," Melville wrote, "all tribes
and people are forming into one federated whole." The notion
"federated," here as in *The Federalist,* is central to the American core concept. A federation is a covenant, something to be
faithful to (from the Latin *foedus,* a cognate of *fides,* "faith")

between diverse and independent states or persons. The model of a federation of independent states was fundamental from the start and applies also to its independent citizens and to groups that are faithful to the core American creed. The Founders did not always refer to our federation as a "nation"; they also called it an "empire."[19] We are no nation in a narrow, innate, nativist sense. It is still fruitful to think of America as the Founders did, as an internal empire. Melville's last remark—"the language they speak shall be the language of Britain"—is central to the whole scheme. I will turn to the subject of language in the next chapter. Meanwhile, there are some key themes to be kept in mind as we move from the core ideas of Madison and Lincoln to the specific aims of American schooling—the foundational distinction between the public and private spheres, the traditional aim of offering children equal educational opportunity, and the critical distinction between nationalism and patriotism.

Public and Private

As early as 1753, Ben Franklin worried about all the different groups that were settling here. He did not foresee that in a few decades, he and his colleagues would write a Constitution that would accommodate everyone, even the Germans.

> Now they come in droves, and carry all before them,
> except in one or two Counties; Few of their children
> in the Country learn English; they import many Books
> from Germany; and of the six printing houses in the
> Province, two are entirely German, two half German

half English, and but two entirely English; They have one German News-paper, and one half German. Advertisements intended to be general are now printed in Dutch and English; the Signs in our Streets have inscriptions in both languages, and in some places only German: They begin of late to make all their Bonds and other legal Writings in their own Language, which (though I think it ought not to be) are allowed good in our Courts, where the German Business so encreases that there is continual need of Interpreters; and I suppose in a few years they will be also necessary in the Assembly, to tell one half of our Legislators what the other half say.[20]

The general principle of the core curriculum is that we deal with different nationalities as we deal with different religions: we leave them alone but expect them to accommodate themselves to the public sphere. Schools are the institution that will enable everybody to make that accommodation. The distinction between the public and private spheres is of course too simple to be fully descriptive of any human social organization.[21] All such categories, including the more refined ones of historians and sociologists, are too simple. The public-private distinction is a regulative idea, that is, an idea that helps us organize and conceptualize our understandings. One of its special virtues is that, as much as any system of description we could apply, it actually animated the creators of the United States. Washington, for instance, saw education as a way of elevating a more expansive public sense of obligation over local and private interests: "A general and liberal diffucion of learn-

ing could be dissiminated, systematically, through all parts of this rising empire; thereby, and as far as the nature of the thing will admit and in itself would be proper, to do away local attachments, and State prejudices from our public councels."²²
Just as our political system is bifurcated—the states on one side and the federal government on the other—so are its citizens separated into various public and private polarities, with the core public sphere being the federation itself.

In 1916 Randolph Bourne published an evocative article in the *Atlantic Monthly* entitled "Trans-National America." In it he proposed that as a nation of immigrants we are all hybrid Americans.

> The Anglo-Saxon was merely the first immigrant, the first to found a colony. He has never really ceased to be the descendant of immigrants, nor has he ever succeeded in transforming that colony into a real nation, with a tenacious, richly woven fabric of native culture. Colonials from the other nations have come and settled down beside him. They found no definite native culture which should startle them out of their colonialism, and consequently they looked back to their mother-country, as the earlier Anglo-Saxon immigrant was looking back to his. What has been offered the newcomer has been the chance to learn English, to become a citizen, to salute the flag. And those elements of our ruling classes who are responsible for the public schools, the settlements, all the organizations for amelioration in the cities, have every reason to be proud. . . .

Do we not begin to see a new and more adventurous ideal? Do we not see how the national colonies in America, deriving power from the deep cultural heart of Europe and yet living here in mutual toleration, freed from the age-long tangles of races, creeds, and dynasties, may work out a federated ideal? Its colonies live here inextricably mingled, yet not homogeneous. They merge but they do not fuse. Whatever American nationalism turns out to be, we see already that it will have color richer and more exciting than our ideal has hitherto encompassed. In a world which has dreamed of internationalism, we find that we have all unawares been building up the first international nation. No Americanization will fulfill this vision which does not recognize the uniqueness of this transnationalism of ours.[23]

Bourne celebrated German-Americans and Italian-Americans as being just as American as English-Americans. And he praised the schools for conveying what the *American* side of the hyphen consists of. He could have carried this cosmopolitan idea even further to include Catholic-Americans, Muslim-Americans, Jewish-Americans, and gay-Americans. He could have included Tennessee-Americans, California-Americans, and New York-Americans, and Philadelphia-Americans and St. Louis-Americans. He could have included African-Americans, Asian-Americans, and not just all races but all associations: the Elks, the AFL-CIO, the American Association of University Women, and the John Birch Society, all with hyphens marking their common allegiance to the core system that offers them freedom and equality and assures their property and safety. They are all comembers of that core "church" and honor its symbol, the flag. Their supertolerant ecumenical "political religion" even tolerates heretical atheist-American flag burners, so long as their actions do not threaten, as Jefferson put it, to pick our pockets or break our legs. The flag burners are hyphenated Americans, too, whether they like it or not. We Americans tolerate a lot of things we do not like, so long as they do no demonstrable injury to us or to the commonweal. When young girls wear headscarves to school we do not, like the French, enter a national crisis. Perhaps that is because France is a nation, whereas we in our public sphere remain, in some hopeful way, transnational.

The concentric circles beyond the systems of communication that we all share, and the core American creed that protects our bodies and our beliefs, our purses and our legs—the circles beyond that core—can be as rich and fulfilling as we are able to make them. Those who press us to create a more substantial American identity need to keep in mind why our core structure was invented in the first place. It was not to build a hearth and a home but to allow us the freedom to build them as we wish, by providing protection from oppression and persecution and bloody wars between rival traditions, tribalisms, and systems of belief. In the present context of fanaticism, this "negative liberty," as the historian Isaiah Berlin calls it, this freedom to be left alone, is all the more precious and attractive. Its principles continue to be, in Lincoln's words, "the last best hope of earth."[24]

Equality and Community

Lincoln uttered the words "the last best hope of earth" in the concluding remarks of his annual address to Congress in December 1862, in the midst of the Civil War. The subject was the freeing of the slaves and the forthcoming Emancipation Proclamation.

> We say we are for the Union. The world will not forget that we say this. We know how to save the Union. The world knows we do know how to save it. We— even we here—hold the power, and bear the responsibility. In giving freedom to the slave, we assure freedom to the free—honorable alike in what we give, and what we preserve. We shall nobly save, or meanly lose, the last best hope of earth. Other means may succeed; this could not fail. The way is plain, peaceful, generous, just—a way which, if followed, the world will forever applaud, and God must forever bless.

Lincoln, to our eternal benefit, understood the meaning of the American experiment as well as any president we have had— better than Teddy Roosevelt or Woodrow Wilson, for example, who did not like the idea of hyphenated Americans. Lincoln saw the American experiment as the last best hope because it was a universalist experiment. It included all persons. Within this inclusiveness, all were bound into one great federation. "Our ancestry is lost in the universal paternity." "We are not a narrow tribe," as Melville put it. The European idea of a nation implies *natio,* descent—*Blut und Boden,* blood and soil. Our transnational idea implies universality. Nothing brings this contrast more urgently to the fore than race, because other than sex, no set of characteristics announces itself to the psyche more forcefully than race—*this person is from a different tribe.* Lincoln did not free white indentured servants; he freed black slaves. If America could begin to conquer the psychological barrier of race, then that would confirm the last best hope of earth, the novel political attempt to transcend tribal hatreds.[25]

Before the nation existed there was the tribe. The history of tribal and racial hatreds is the history and prehistory of humankind. Our insight into the universal phenomenon of tribalism has deepened since the advent of evolutionary psychology, whose speculations make us realize how natural are the group hatreds and cruelties of history resisted by the artificial constructs of civilization.[26] Tribalism is natural to humans because the tribal instinct has been highly adaptive in primate evolution. Humans need to live in groups. We are social animals. Tribalism helps keep individuals within the group committed to the cooperative sphere needed for group survival. A key element of this commitment is the common enemy. If things begin to fall apart within the group, its leaders can often restore unity by starting a war or scapegoating another group. One form of tribalism—religious persecution—was the version of this evil that our political religion was designed to nullify. Tribalism is still the human race's deadliest means of self-destruction. The American experiment, which now seems so natural to us, is a thoroughly artificial device designed to counterbalance the natural impulses of group suspicions and hatreds.

Our brilliant political tradition cannot altogether remove the instinct of tribalism, with its innate dislike and suspicion of the other, but it is the best system yet devised for counteracting it, for transforming an *other* into an *us*. Under our political religion the sense of the group has gradually been made more expansive, so that race, gender, temperament, and religion cease to be core group characteristics and are relegated to the private sphere. The ineradicable instinct of tribal hostility toward the other can then be channeled into harmless sports rivalries and fan affiliations. The American flag, symbol of the "political religion" of the group, has been useful in enhancing American group solidarity on a vast scale. But the main agencies of group solidarity in large countries are two: a common language and a common education into the group's core mores and loyalties.[27] This vast, artificial, transtribal construct is what our Founders aimed to achieve. And they understood that it can be achieved effectively only by intelligent schooling. As Horace Mann stated, distinctions of tribe and caste can be overcome only by an education that fosters equality and thereby brings everyone into the *same* group.

Equality—both equality before the law and equality of opportunity—is therefore not only a core American value but also a core requisite for a peaceable public sphere. In America, universal schooling has always been understood as critical to our ideal of equality. In the introduction to his 1817 bill for an Elementary School Act in Virginia, the aging Thomas Jefferson, the most consistent of the Founders in stressing the importance of public education, succinctly stated the grounds for equality of opportunity. An educational system that offered it would "avail the commonwealth of those talents and virtues which nature has sown as liberally among the poor as rich."[28]

David McCullough has observed that Jefferson lived like an aristocrat but talked like an egalitarian, whereas John Adams lived like a plain citizen but argued for a "natural aristocracy." In the 1813 correspondence between the two men, Adams proposed that the nation should encourage a quasi-aristocracy of good families who were devoted to the public good. Jefferson, coming on his mother's side from the best of families (the Randolphs) and being well positioned to know how variable were their issue, was more disdainful of such "pseudo aristocracy." He desired "to bring into action that mass of talents which lies buried in poverty."[29] He was animated not just by a sense of fairness but also by a desire that the Republic make use of those with greatest talent and virtue. "For I agree with you that there is a natural aristocracy among men. The grounds of this are virtue and talents. . . . There is also an artificial aristocracy founded on wealth and birth, without either virtue or talents; . . . The natural aristocracy I consider as the most precious gift of nature for the instruction, the trusts, and government of society. . . . The artificial aristocracy is a mischievous ingredient in government, and provision should be made to prevent its ascendancy."[30]

Jefferson was proud that immediately after the Declaration of Independence, the first laws he pushed through the Virginia legislature were designed to abolish the remnants of aristocracy. First he sponsored a law abolishing entail—the ability of the dead through their wills to control the actions of their living. Next he sponsored a law abolishing primogeniture—the tradition of leaving one's estate to the firstborn and thereby preserving vast wealth in single hands. The children of each generation should start out on an equal footing, neither constrained by entail nor elevated by greatly unequal distributions of wealth.

The Jeffersonian ideal gave rise to the hope and, in many cases, the reality of a mobile and meritocratic society. "The American Dream" connotes a rags-to-riches story that inspired and fulfilled generations of Americans. Many such stories are still to be told today. America still offers "a career open to talents," but perhaps it is less open today, when achieving honor or wealth requires higher levels of education. Our schools have not been adequately developing "the talents and virtues which nature has sown as liberally among the poor as rich," as may be seen from this chart.

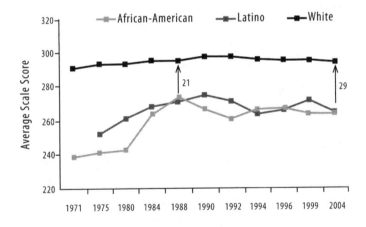

NAEP reading, seventeen-year-olds. Source: National Center for Education Statistics, NAEP 2004 Trends in Academic Progress. Courtesy The Core Knowledge Foundation

With such persistent inequalities it will be impossible truly to overcome our tribalisms and group resentments or achieve a greater sense of solidarity among our citizens. As I will show in chapter 5, the kind of education that will lead to general competence and enable this sense of solidarity is precisely the kind that will narrow the unfortunate gaps among demographic groups.

Loyalty versus Jingoism

In his superb, evocative study of nationalism, *Imagined Communities*, Benedict Anderson wrote admiringly of American schooling that "the son of an Italian immigrant to New York will find ancestors in the Pilgrim Fathers."[31] But long before Anderson published his book (in 1983), this sense of imaginatively shared history was receding and was no longer being effectively instilled by American schools. The invented sense of a shared past based on the historical ideals of the United States was being replaced by an invented sense of a shared past in some other remote place or culture. As a consequence, many young Americans began seeking their roots in imagined ancestral pasts rather than an imagined American community. The television series *Roots* was a hugely popular television success. My young nephews, brought up, like me, in Memphis, Tennessee, as nonobservant Reform Jews, suddenly reinvented themselves in the 1970s as orthodox, ritualistic, Hebrew-learning sectarians. They had found their roots.

None of these new filiations, of course, was any more or less invented than America itself, as it was presented by the schools in the mid-nineteenth and early twentieth centuries.

The same can be said of the pieties of recent group identities in self-conscious "multiculturalism."[32] The retrograde move toward neotribalism by young people fulfills a psychological need that has been at least partly created by our schools' failure to continue making our glorious idea of a supertribe into the inspiring creed that Lincoln urged them to promote.[33] That creed has been and should remain an inspiring element of early schooling.

In chapter 2 I explained how, by the early twentieth century, Americans had become so self-confident that educators grew complacent about the psychological difficulty of sustaining community feeling in a vast, heterogeneous country. They took for granted the inherited patriotism of Americans and the cohesiveness of the Republic. The child-centered education they advocated found a response in the wider American community. Parents, brought up on William Wordsworth and Ralph Waldo Emerson, shared the progressives' confidence in the United States and in the inherent goodness of human nature, rather than taking Lincoln's and the Founders' far more cautious view. The individualistic orientation of the new educational ideas seemed to hold no dangers, only promise. The early decades of the twentieth century saw a gradual diminishment in schoolbooks of the "civic religion" approach to American political institutions and heroes.[34]

The more recent idea that our political religion is made somehow obsolete by globalism overlooks the point that the United States was a global democracy from the start: the world has followed the pattern that we set. The colonies, with their internal multiple identities, were made global by the sailing ship, multilingual by the printing press, and multicultural by the steamship and the railroad and then the radio, airplane, television, computer, and Internet. These technologies hastened the spread of America's internal multiple identities but did not change the underlying cosmopolitan pattern. Robert Frost wrote, "I am overtired / Of the great harvest I myself desired." The cosmopolitan democracy created by eighteenth-century intellectuals enabled America to become multicultural, middle-browed, and anti-intellectual.[35] When the egalitarianism of the elite Founders became a reality, it produced a world that scorned elitism and became, in some quarters, hostile even to the Founders themselves.[36] So successful has been the American experiment that it has sown the seeds of its own faltering as a human community. The universalistic, cosmopolitan principles on which it is based cannot easily replace the warm group loyalties that bind together narrower, more tribal groups connected by ties of kinship and shared memory. Despite that profound difficulty, America has nonetheless been able to sustain a remarkable loyalty and patriotism among its citizens by means of its civil religion, just as Lincoln so powerfully urged it to do in his Lyceum address. Being universalistic, that civil religion is antagonistic to racism, sexism, jingoism, or injustice. When America falls short of its own ideals, idealistic Americans can become anti-American.[37]

The intellectual and moral error of some members of the intellectual elite has been to equate American patriotism with narrow nationalism and militaristic flag-waving.[38] They have a point. When the Nazis came to power in Germany in the 1930s, there was a flowering of German flags and a sharp rise of government-induced patriotic fervor. But the special character of *that* kind of nationalism has little to do with the more accommodating American patriotism. The best writer on this subject is Benedict Anderson, who sees this hostile form of nationalistic flag-waving as tribalism—always directed against some other tribe: the Jews, the Blacks, the Muslims, the Hispanics, and so on. Anderson connects this whipped-up nationalism with racism, an attempt to resist or overcome some other group.[39] The language is that of "contamination" or "infiltration." Real patriotism, he observes, involves a willingness to sacrifice and even die for the patria and defines itself not by its difference from or superiority to some "other" but rather by its unconditional loyalty. It was this disinterested, nonmilitaristic form of patriotism that George Washington tried to exemplify when, against all expectations after our military victory that he would become the de facto king of America, he resigned his commission as commander in chief and returned to his farm—an act that (as he intended) had an enormous impact on not only his compatriots but the world.

The true American form of patriotism is commodious rather than tribal. It is inherently cosmopolitan—the first such patriotism in the history of the world and, in that respect, at its best, a beacon. But America also has content; it is not an unrooted polyglot cosmopolitanism. It accommodates all groups but at the same time, through commonalities and principles learned in childhood, fills the human need for group attachment—the noblest such political experiment yet attempted. The proper aim of American schools is not jingoism but loyalty to a truly glorious ideal. As Anderson observes, such loyalty to an imagined community can be accomplished only through a common language. Commonality of language is the indispensable vehicle of loyalty and solidarity as well as general competence. Language, like the civic ideals of freedom, equality, and toleration, is thus at the center of the core curriculum.

> Amor patria [love of country] does not differ in this respect from other affections in which there is always an element of fond imagining. . . . What the eye is to the lover—that particular, ordinary eye he or she was born with—language—whatever language history has made his or her mother tongue—is to the patriot. Through that language, encountered at mother's knee and parted with only at the grave, pasts are restored, fellowships are imagined, and futures dreamed.[40]

4

Linguistic America and the Public Sphere

Lincoln mentioned schoolbooks in a speech already quoted: "Let reverence for the laws, be breathed by every American mother, to the lisping babe, that prattles on her lap—let it be taught in schools, in seminaries, and in colleges;—let it be written in Primmers, spelling books." Primers and spelling books have always been understood to have a larger goal than just imparting the secrets of the written code. They are also meant to impart some of the common knowledge and values that accompany language use in the public sphere. The first textbook of the American colonies, the Puritans' *New England Primer* of the 1680s, did not say, "A is for *Apple*." It said, "In *Adam's* fall, we sin-ned all." The schools have been responsible for teaching children not only the standard written and oral code but also some of the underlying assumptions that go with its use. A goal of the common school is to teach the common language so that all can participate in the public sphere.

For some American children, the standard print code is the language they speak at home. But for other children it is not, and this has led to resentful charges of language imperialism. American schools have thus been caught up in controversies that have paralyzed textbook writers, teachers, and administrators even beyond the laissez-faire approach to the print code recommended by some in the anti-curriculum movement. The last time I spoke with Albert Shanker, shortly before he died, we were guests on a radio program discussing whether the schools should teach a dialect called "Ebonics" to African-American students. Al and I were the lone dissenters. I politely mentioned some technical objections. He simply said, "It's a terrible idea." Among educators, only Al had the courage to be so blunt. I will try to explain why he was right, not just on that score but on a host of issues concerning the teaching of "language arts."

The Public Sphere and the Linguistic Commons

Early on, the anti-curriculum movement advocated natural methods of teaching reading—"the whole-word method," which later morphed into the "whole-language" method with the claim that immersion in authentic language experiences would lead students to translate written symbols into sounds more successfully than the artificial study of phonics. A natural approach, the theory said, will unerringly lead to the right result. During the past two decades the National Institutes of Health have exploded this idea through exhaustive research, but not before hundreds thousands of students had been consigned to semiliteracy. Teachers now say that the recent science has simply driven the whole-language movement underground. It has adopted a new label, "balanced literacy," but to the extent that it neglects systematic phonics, it still fails to teach the decoding of letters into language sounds.

The teaching of grammar also came under attack from the natural-is-best movement, which sponsored many studies purporting to show the ineffectiveness of grammar study.[1] Today, most state standards in language arts do not require children to learn the parts of speech in the early grades. Prospective teachers are told in authoritative tones that linguistics has proved the inadvisability of teaching correct pronunciation and grammar. Such views, conveyed in teacher manuals, might be labeled "providential linguistics": Don't worry: language is natural; all will work out for the best. One distinguished psychologist commented, "If a small part of the research effort that has been put into demonstrating the uselessness of grammar . . . had been distributed over a wider field, more might be known about how skill in the use of English can best be developed."[2] In view of widespread misconceptions about standard grammar and standard language, in this chapter I will try to provide very briefly some linguistic background regarding Standard American Written English. This information is not being transmitted to the elementary schoolteachers who need it most.

A beginning teacher recently complained in print about the harm that lack of guidance was doing to her professional life and to her students:

> What grammar should I be teaching them? Capitalization? Punctuation? Sentence structure? What have my students already learned and what will they be ex-

pected to know by the end of the year when I pass them along to the next teacher? . . . Besides putting students at a great disadvantage, particularly those who transfer classes or schools mid-year, the lack of clearly defined expectations adds an enormous amount of work and stress to my life. Since becoming a teacher my entire existence has revolved around a single, haunting question, "What am I going to teach next?"[3]

College teachers report that when students actually make it to college, they do not write or spell adequately. Heather Macdonald gives an example in *City Journal:*

> The following short essay—reprinted here verbatim—received an A in [CCNY's] English 110, a nonremedial course. (It answers the question: "What advice would you give Charles about memorizing data and passing tests?")
> I would tell Charles to read and then don't just stop and go do some thing else but to rectie and don't lay in you bed and say you are studying but to move up and down and rectie. I would also tell him to do overlearning because the more you overlearn something you will be able to remembrance on a test. he can also use scheme that could help you to remembrance a lot more.

Student writing has become so bad that it defeats the impulse to improve it. Al Fiellin, a former dean of

City's General Education and Guidance Division, discovered that remedial writing students were losing through disuse whatever skills they had acquired in remediation. So he tried to introduce a very modest writing requirement into all core curriculum courses. He met with widespread faculty resistance. The typical response to his proposal was: "I have too many students who can't write well enough for me to help." Short-answer and multiple-choice tests have become the preferred evaluation method, so that faculty members can avoid having to read student papers.[4]

How did we reach this pass? In the early 1970s, two important organizations for teaching the English language in the United States, the Conference on College Composition and Communication and the National Council of Teachers of English, put out a well-intentioned but muddled resolution called *Students' Right to Their Own Language.* The resolution reads as follows:

> We affirm the students' right to their own patterns and varieties of language—the dialects of their nurture or whatever dialects in which they find their own identity and style. Language scholars long ago denied that the myth of a standard American dialect has any validity. The claim that any one dialect is unacceptable amounts to an attempt of one social group to exert its dominance over another. Such a claim leads to false advice for speakers and writers, and immoral advice for humans. A nation proud of its diverse heritage and

its cultural and racial variety will preserve its heritage of dialects. We affirm strongly that teachers must have the experiences and training that will enable them to respect diversity and uphold the right of students to their own language.[5]

The organizations reaffirmed this resolution in 2003.

I once saw a sign that said, "The trouble with a half truth is that you might have hold of the wrong half." The honorable impulse behind the resolution is that teachers should not make students feel that their home speech is somehow unworthy. But that is all it should have said. The rest is simply incorrect, and I am embarrassed that two organizations I once belonged to are still supporting this factually inadmissible and ethically suspect resolution. The leaders of these organizations should check up on these claims, especially the assertion that "language scholars long ago denied that the myth of a standard American dialect has any validity," the most ill-informed public statement by a learned society in many years. Mainstream linguistic scholarship recognizes that standard American English is no myth. It is the language of your local newspaper, radio station, and favorite blog. The standard language is one of the firmest and most stable realities of American life.

Moreover, the standard language is the great organ of economic competence, social equality, and solidarity. Even if one argues (incorrectly) that there is no standard American dialect but only a dialect of "power," to restrict students' mastery of that dialect is to deny them access to power, as Gramsci and others after him have observed. By refusing to teach it explicitly, we deny children a vital tool that they need to participate fully in civic activity, make their voices heard, and make their grievances felt. We limit their job prospects and economic viability and sentence them to a life of harsh judgments from members of the broader speech community about their intelligence and abilities, based solely on their inability to communicate in the standard dialect. By equating the teaching of a standard American dialect with oppression and by refusing to give students the linguistic tools they need to be full participants in society, we are in fact oppressing them.

This is the insight powerfully offered by Lisa Delpit in her well-named book *Other People's Children.* As an African-American educator, Delpit is sensitive to the schools' duty to empower students with the standard language. The implication of her title is that while it's all very well to pronounce that students have a right to their own language, sensible parents will certainly want their *own* children to wield the standard language effectively. The conventions of the standard language and the taken-for-granted knowledge that accompanies its use should be taught explicitly. Delpit says, "If such explicitness is not provided to students, what it feels like to people who are old enough to judge is that there are secrets being kept, that time is being wasted, that the teacher is abdicating his or her duty to teach."[6]

Just as Jefferson did not care what gods his neighbors might privately worship, he would not have cared what language or dialect they might speak at home. But whatever language Americans speak in the private sphere, they need to use Standard English in the public sphere, not just for practical economic purposes but also to facilitate communication and decision making in a democracy. Gordon S. Wood reminds us that the American Founders preferred a common language not just for practical reasons but also to support ideals of civility, mutual respect, and goodwill:

> Since civilization was something that could be achieved, everything was enlisted in order to push back barbarism and ignorance and spread civility and refinement. Courtesy books that told Americans how to behave doubled in numbers. . . . Compilers of dictionaries attempted to find the correct meanings, spellings, and punctuations of words, and freeze them between the covers of their books. In these ways peculiarities of dialect, and eccentricities of spelling and pronunciation could be eliminated, and standards of the language could be set. . . . [Being a gentleman] meant being reasonable, tolerant, honest, virtuous, and "candid." . . . It signified being cosmopolitan. . . . It meant, in short, having all those characteristics that we today sum up in the idea of a liberal arts education.[7]

Who are the present-day enemies of these inspiring ideals who issue self-righteous resolutions against central educational responsibilities? Mainly they are academic theorists, whose argument runs like this: The supposedly universalist ideals of civility and a common language are really the history-bound prejudices of a dominant class—the white, Anglo-Saxon bourgeoisie who seek to impose their values and language on those who have different sets of values or different dialects. Their supposedly classless society is really the imperialistic imposition of a particular social class and language group. But other languages and customs are just as valid as theirs. This idea is, of course, quintessentially American. But I have been struck by a hidden feature of this argument: It is put forward by people who express themselves within the very language norms that their argument repudiates. Such manifestos are never phrased in nonstandard language, always in Standard English. That does not in itself invalidate the argument, but a further implication does: If the argument for non-standard language were made in nonstandard language, no one would pay serious attention. The assertion of students' right to their own language therefore amounts to this: "You have no right to insist that American students be taught to write or speak in the only way that other Americans will pay serious attention to." Self-righteous ideologues who call the standard American language a mere class dialect are simply one more faction within the multifarious fabric of the whole, and like everyone else who commands attention in the public sphere, they conduct their agitations in the very language they condemn.

The standard American language is not a class dialect, nor is the standard knowledge that underlies it the property of a subgroup. The standard language is an artificial construct, created over centuries, that has become so fixed that its basic structure is unlikely to change no matter what group or ideology is in charge. Both Standard English and the knowledge that enables its use are the property of all. Universal mastery of them is essential to real democracy. Only those who master that language and its coordinate knowledge are full participants in the linguistic commons and the public sphere.

How the American Language Got Standardized

The idea that the standard language is a mere class dialect got started because historical linguists pointed out that the original forms of language that ultimately became standardized were forms spoken in the courts of British monarchs. But to pay too much attention to dialectal origins is to commit the genetic fallacy—the assumption that the genesis of a thing limits and defines its later character. In the case of language in the modern world it is a plausible mistake, since you cannot belong to the top group these days unless you can read, write, and speak the standard language.

Whose dialect *did* become the American language? Nobody's. By the time the United States was forming into a nation, we had inherited this artificial construct from the language standardizers of England. Hence the short and simple answer to the question "How did the American language get standardized?" is straightforward. We took over from the English a language that was already standardized. Noah Webster's spelling book and dictionary offered but slight deviations from Dr. Johnson's dictionary. The English had followed the pattern that was followed everywhere else: they made dictionaries and grammar books, instituted schools that taught the authoritative decisions, and waited a few generations. When almost all children attend schools where they are taught the "correct" forms of syntax, grammar, spelling, and pronunciation, the print code becomes, after some generations, the language spoken in the public sphere, and often at the mother's knee.[8]

The standard language then becomes very resistant to change. This stability is a key point that gets glossed over in the language popularizations teachers normally see. Dictionary compilers, who put out new editions every decade or so, tell us how much our language has changed in the intervening span. They explain that new words and the things they represent—*DVDs, satellite radio, Bollywood, blog*—are coming into currency, while other words and acronyms such as *BVDs* (not *DVDs*) are disappearing along with the things they represent.[9] Such vocabulary change is a fascinating subject, but ever since the late nineteenth century, new words have occupied a surprisingly small segment of the English vocabulary, and grammar has hardly changed at all.

On a table in my study is the massive Webster's *New International Dictionary of the English Language,* dated 1934. It contains over three thousand large pages, holding around a hundred definitions each. It lacks, of course, all the post-1934 coinages, but it nonetheless remains, after seventy-five years, a reliable guide to almost any word I have wished to look up. No doubt a new dictionary would contain useful recent additions, but there is good reason to believe that in 2034, when my current one is a hundred years old, it will still be a reliable guide to the main meanings of its three hundred thousand words, and their spellings and pronunciations. There's an even stronger reason to believe that the spelling, pronunciation, grammar, and syntax used in its definitions will be current after another hundred years, in 2134. The conservatism of language is great once its standard forms are set down in dictionaries and taught in school. It is reinforced not just by growing use but also by all the books and magazines and blogs that come out each day and collect in the library. Such stability, still relatively new in the history of language, owes its origin to the standardizing role of the printing press in disseminating the written word to increasingly large segments of the public. In the early eighteenth century, just before language standardization became dominant in England, Alexander Pope worried that he would not be understood after sixty years because of what language change had done to English writers before him. "Short is the Date, alas, of Modern Rhymes," Pope mournfully wrote in 1711:

And 'tis but just to let 'em live betimes.
No longer now that Golden Age appears,
When Patriarch-Wits surviv'd a thousand Years;
Now Length of Fame (our second Life) is lost,
And bare Threescore is all ev'n That can boast.[10]

According to this math, his own writings would soon be unreadable, and like his contemporary John Dryden, he would end up sounding to future readers as Chaucer sounds to us— like some strange foreign tongue: "Our Sons their Fathers' failing language see, / And such as Chaucer is, shall Dryden be."[11] But because Pope was lucky enough to flourish at the start of the era of language standardization, American schoolchildren of today can read these very lines. The linguist Henry Bradley, one of the editors of the great *New English Dictionary on Historical Principles,* deserves credit for first predicting the stability of the newly standardized languages. In 1904 he wrote, "On the whole it is probable that the history of English grammar will for a very long time have few changes to record later than the nineteenth century."[12]

He might have said "later than the eighteenth century," the era when our Republic arose fully formed in a linguistic sense. Our founding documents, the Declaration of Independence and the Constitution, are written and spelled in essentially our own language: "We the People of the United States, in Order to form a more perfect Union, establish Justice, insure domestic Tranquility, provide for the common defense, promote the general Welfare, and secure the Blessings of Liberty to ourselves and our Posterity, do ordain and establish this Constitution for the United States of America."

The United States was born in the era of language standardization and universal literacy. It is the very child of literacy and schooling. In an earlier time, Pope would have been right about the impermanence of language. Mutability had always been its fate, and it still is wherever the language exists only in oral form. If one goes back far enough in time to the era before mass literacy, the language of one's ancestors looks like gibberish. We take for granted that our Constitution is intelligible, but Britons' earlier legal code is simply unintelligible to all but scholars of Old English:

> Of ðissum anum dome mon mæg geðencean, þæt he æghwelcne on ryht gedemeð; ne ðearf he nanra domboca oþerra. Geðence he, þæt he nanum men ne deme þæt he nolde ðæt he him demde, gif he ðone dom ofer hine sohte.[13]

Dialects varied over space as well as time. Before mass literacy, local dialects were so distinct that the historical linguist Angus Macintosh used to say he could identify within twenty miles where a premodern British manuscript had been written. Dialects a hundred miles apart were mutually unintelligible.[14]

The United States happened to be founded, then, on the cusp of a deep change in human affairs: the post-Gutenberg rise of the modern industrial nation and large-scale early schooling. Industrialization was accompanied by the self-conscious standardization of national languages, usually through national academies. The newly developing nations depended for their effective functioning on an expansion of literacy and communication among all citizens, no matter how far they might be from the centers of political and economic power.[15] Throughout Britain, France, Germany, Spain, and the United States, schools were instituted to teach reading and writing in the new national tongues. Such imposition of language uniformity over big geographical stretches, central to the modern world, was something new in human experience.[16] Without language standardization spread by universal schooling, the economic and political network that is the modern nation could not exist.

In sum, since the beginning of the United States in the late eighteenth century, schools have had a duty to make every child conversant with the spoken and written forms of Standard English. The forms themselves have remained stable since the founding, and they transcend class: schools have had the duty to bring them to all classes of society. Children who have not been properly taught the stable, standard forms can never belong to the top tier of society. This point cannot be too strongly emphasized, because organizations like the National

Council of Teachers of English have recently associated standard language with social class. Whatever apparent validity this association has today is altogether contingent. Well-off people, with fewer and fewer exceptions as time passes, tend to be able to deploy the standard language. But is this because well-off people belong to the class that deploys Standard English, or is it because deploying Standard English is increasingly a prerequisite to being well-off? That the latter is the more likely explanation is suggested by listening to army generals. Many of them came from humble origins and rose by merit within the military—our most meritocratic institution. All generals speak and write Standard English in the public sphere. If they did not, they would not be generals.

Teaching Students How to Use the Standard Language

In its grammatical forms and spellings, American English is not very different from British English. While George Bernard Shaw's wisecrack about the two nations being separated by a common language has an element of truth, it has almost nothing to do with grammar and spelling and everything to do with tacit knowledge. The assumed knowledge of the British public sphere is different from that of the American public sphere. And it is this unspoken knowledge that chiefly makes the American language American. It is true that the vocabularies in the two countries are also slightly different. I remember being puzzled, the year we lived in London, that a swimming competition for our children was called a "gala." But such vagaries are rare; the real difference in the two speech communities lies in what is silently taken for granted—as anyone can confirm by going online to read a British newspaper. There it will quickly be observed, through occasional puzzling passages, that unstated knowledge is critical to understanding what is being stated. To write is to communicate one's meaning to an unknown, unseen reader. To read is to be able to understand what some unseen writer desired to communicate. Communication is at the center of reading and writing, and it takes place in a context of shared, unspoken knowledge and values. To enable all children to communicate in the standard language, the unspoken knowledge that is taken for granted in newspapers and books is precisely what must *not* be taken for granted in school. On the contrary, the unspoken knowledge that is assumed in writing addressed to the general public must be made explicit and imparted to all.

This observation does not devalue teaching the mechanics of literacy. Learning them is an immense intellectual task for a young child. Thanks to the scientific work sponsored by the National Institutes of Health and publicized by the National Reading Panel, the systematic teaching of alphabetic reading and writing is a frontier that our schools have begun to cross. Schools are settling into the pastures of "phonemic awareness," "blending," and the rest. But while the teaching of phonics has our children advancing in reading scores in the early grades, where the mechanics of reading are the main things probed on reading tests, they are not advancing in the later grades, when the tests' main focus is language *comprehension*.

The NEAP assessment of students' reading scores over three decades, reproduced here, contains the principal data

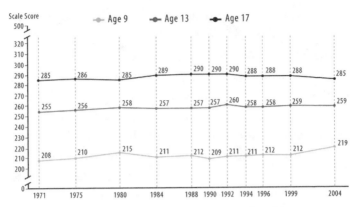

Student reading scores, 1971–2004, ages nine, thirteen, and seventeen. Source: National Assessment of Educational Progress. Courtesy The Core Knowledge Foundation

one needs to know about the recent state of American education. Despite many earnest efforts and reforms, despite a massive effort at improving reading under No Child Left Behind, students who leave school at the end of our K-12 education cannot read, learn, or communicate very well, whether measured by international standards or our own.[17] That is because the schools are not effectively imparting the knowledge that the effective use of standard language depends on. This knowledge has to be just as deliberately transmitted by the schools as phonemic awareness and blending.[18]

Communication across wide distances is today a central feature of reading and writing and speaking—all the more so with e-mail and the Internet. For an author, predicting what an unknown, unseen audience can be expected to know is a key task of writing, whether in a newspaper or a fourth-grade classroom exercise. If schools have an obligation to teach reading and writing, it follows that they must also teach students how to communicate with an unknown and unseen audience. Writers (or speakers) at every level have to understand what they can take for granted and what they must explain.

A dimension of unstated knowledge is a universal characteristic of language. When President Richard Nixon taped his Oval Office conversations, he left behind a trove of linguistic evidence showing how much is silently assumed in the speech of small groups. Transcripts of the Nixon Watergate tapes were in many places simply incomprehensible until scholars surrounded the text with a lot of this necessary information.

SHULTZ: I talked with Meany this afternoon about the SST.

PRESIDENT: What'd he say?

SHULTZ: He said he was all out on it. If there was anything we wanted him to do, he wanted to do it. He'd be ready to do it. They—

PRESIDENT: Well, could you ask him to, could you ask him, could you phone him back after this meeting and ask him to call Hubert Humphrey, with the understanding he, uh—

SHULTZ: Yeah.[19]

Even before we get to this particular bit of dialogue, let's unpack just a few of the unstated things a reader has to know even to make sense of my introduction of it. Richard Nixon was a recent Republican president. He resigned in part because the conversations that he secretly taped at the White House revealed that he was part of a criminal conspiracy to break into the Democratic National Headquarters to gain an advantage in the 1972 presidential election. The headquarters were in the Watergate Hotel complex in Washington, DC, and so the scandal was called "Watergate" and the tapes were called "the Nixon Tapes" or "the Watergate Tapes." In those days, audio recordings were made on magnetic tape. They were made public by court order. All this must be understood before a reader can even begin to wonder who Meany was, what the SST was, what Nixon and his budget director, George P. Shultz, were hoping to accomplish, who Hubert Humphrey was, and why Nixon thought it would help if Meany talked with him.

Of course, for those who do not know about presidential elections, audio recordings, court orders, and so on, the gloss I gave above would need to be glossed further. All verbal communication takes a vast amount of relevant background information for granted. What is a president? What is a Republican? Where to start? To make written communication reasonably efficient, a good deal of relevant knowledge must already be shared between interlocutors. The more they share, the briefer the utterance can be.

What language conventions and knowledge do students have to master to meet their fellow citizens as equals on the linguistic commons? Such questions seem hard to answer in the abstract, because so much depends on the specific topic and audience. But there *is* effective communication to general audiences in the public sphere. The problem of shared, taken-for-granted knowledge has, as a practical fact, been solved. Those who successfully communicate to a wide audience are able to do so because the public dimension of shared knowledge is, at any given time, implicitly standardized like the other conventions of language. Standard language goes with standard knowledge in the public sphere. This shared knowledge changes, of course. To belong to the speech community of the United States today you need some basic knowledge of, say, baseball. Suppose a friend asks me about last night's game, and I say, "We won—one to nothing. Sampson sacrificed and knocked in a run in the bottom of the ninth." This statement would puzzle most Britons. Most Americans would not only understand the basic meaning but could construct a "situation model." They could infer that there were fewer than two outs, that a runner was probably on third, that the sacrifice hit was a longish fly rather than a bunt, that there was a lot of noise from the stands, and that the game ended right there without another at-bat. All that and much more can be conveyed to an American in the words "Samson sacrificed and knocked in a run in the bottom of the ninth."

But take another example that both a Briton and an American would certainly understand, one of the most famous sentences in English literature: "It is a truth universally acknowledged that a single man in possession of a good fortune must be in want of a wife." Imagine inexperienced readers, say eleven-year-olds, reading that opening sentence of *Pride and Prejudice* and taking the words at face value. They think, "Okay, the author believes that everybody knows that truth." If young readers don't comprehend Jane Austen's irony, it would not be because they lacked humor or subtlety but because they lacked knowledge. All irony depends on unspoken knowledge and attitudes shared between speaker and listener, between writer and reader (if the attitudes are not unspoken, the statement can hardly be ironic), and most eleven-year-olds don't know enough for full membership in the Jane Austen speech community. Irony is like baseball talk: it takes a lot of unspoken things for granted. But it is definitely not an elite phenomenon. Rural and city talk are full of irony.[20]

The bottom line is this: To be members of the wider club and to stand as equals on the linguistic commons of the nation, the participants in the public sphere have to share a great deal of unspoken background knowledge. If we want all citizens to be able to participate as equals in that sphere, our schools need to teach all students the required knowledge. The notion that reading comprehension is some sort of formal ability that can be learned by practicing strategy drills on whimsical fictions is a tragic mistake.[21]

Teaching Standard Knowledge

We have moved to the proposition that, in order to enable communication in the public sphere, commonality of language requires commonality of knowledge. Now we need to take the next logical step. Commonality of knowledge requires commonality in schooling. The schools need to impart not only the forms of the standard language but also the unstated knowledge students need in order to understand what is being said in the classroom, in newspapers, and elsewhere in the public sphere. This unstated knowledge is extensive, and it needs to be imparted gradually and securely over the years of schooling. Indeed, the vastness of this knowledge is the chief reason schooling takes so many years. If reading and writing were simply how-to skills, three or four years would suffice. You could graduate after fourth grade. But thirteen years are barely enough to gain the needed general knowledge for mature literacy in the Internet age, and even that many years, as we have seen from the NAEP data, have not sufficed in the United States.

As I mentioned, the tacit knowledge needed for understanding books, newspapers, and blogs is more or less standardized in a given era. This is a technical necessity. If I as a writer cannot predict what my unseen audience already knows, then I cannot know how to communicate with it. The example of the White House tapes illustrates how this shared knowledge changes. Knowledge of the Watergate scandal obviously could not have been taken for granted before 1972, and it will surely not be shared a few decades in the future. But, remarkably enough, readers of today *can* understand Jane Austen and other nineteenth-century novelists, and they can understand the themes of the Declaration of Independence. Clearly, some of the tacit knowledge needed for reading comprehension has a longer shelf life than the White House tapes. In deciding on the core contents of the school curriculum, it makes sense, therefore, to place stress on the most durable, least ephemeral tacit public knowledge. That was the conscious purpose of Blair's *Rhetoric,* and it explains why the Harvard Library holds 124 editions of that work from 1793 to 1990.

One twentieth-century proponent of this approach was Carleton Washburne, superintendent of schools in Winnetka, Illinois, from 1919 to 1943. He asked what things all children need to know to flourish in American society today and then framed the curriculum around these "common essentials."

Washburne met with disapproval from fellow progressives, who opposed any specific curriculum set in advance. In his innocence, he did not realize that he had transgressed the anti-curriculum principle. In 1987, I ventured to set down an index to some of the knowledge students needed to possess to be proficient in the American standard language.[22] In the two decades since then, my colleagues and I at the Core Knowledge Foundation have transformed that list into a coherent core curriculum that is now being followed by hundreds of schools. Unsurprisingly, reading comprehension scores at these schools have soared.[23]

Other sequences that put the same basic knowledge in a different order could be equally effective. But the substance of any such curriculum would need to be very similar to the Core Knowledge curriculum, because the taken-for-granted knowledge in the American public sphere is finite and definable, and its extent is implicitly known to all who need to communicate in writing within that sphere. Moreover, any effective compilation would need to be, like ours, grade-specific. This is a critical point for the following reasons:

1. Specifying core content by year enables the teacher at each grade level to know what students already know, making it possible to communicate with the whole class and bring the whole group forward. As Harold Stevenson and James Stigler pointed out in their pathbreaking book *The Learning Gap,* the American classroom's lack of productivity is not chiefly caused by diversity of ethnic and family background but by diversity of

academic preparation. Under the anti-curriculum imperium, the disparity in student readiness increases with each successive grade, slowing down progress and making the teacher's task ever more difficult. In core-curriculum nations such as Finland and France, the disparity in student readiness decreases over time.[24]

2. When critical knowledge gaps and boring repetitions are avoided, student interest and motivation are enhanced and progress in learning speeds up. Many American teachers say that they spend several weeks at the start of each year in review. That is, they offer a mini-course in the things students need to know to go forward. To students who already know those things, the review is an occasion to start shooting spitballs. Those who lack the needed knowledge are clueless and throw spitballs, too. No wonder the attrition rate of teachers rises with each successive grade in American schools.

3. Instituting a core of year-by-year commonality among different schools to offer more coherent schooling is especially helpful for disadvantaged students who change schools. By third grade, some 70 percent of low-income students have changed schools, many in the middle of the year.

4. Specific, grade-by-grade planning allows the entire curriculum to be integrated. The history of a

period can be integrated with its art and music. Such integration leads to better retention and fuller understanding.

I have not encountered any cogent counterarguments against these reasons for greater commonality and specificity in the early curriculum—a conclusion I will amplify in the final two chapters.

A Note on Teaching the Grammar of the Standard Language

It is a highly democratic aim to enable everybody to speak and write in the standard forms, to ensure that one's education, brains, or social class will not be disparaged. As Gordon Wood points out, that was a founding, egalitarian ideal of American schooling, an ideal now bedimmed and confounded. We don't have to invent examples of the confused ideas that currently beset our schools' language-arts teachers, who are doing their best. The National Council of Teachers of English and schools of education provide ready-made the examples of bad advice. To go along with the egregious resolution *Students' Right to Their Own Language,* here is the NCTE resolution on grammar: "Resolved, that the National Council of Teachers of English affirm the position that the use of isolated grammar and usage exercises not supported by theory and research is a deterrent to the improvement of students' speaking and writing and that, in order to improve both of these, class time at all levels must be devoted to opportunities for meaningful listening, speaking, reading, and writing; and that NCTE urge the discontinuance of testing practices that encourage the teaching of grammar rather than English language arts instruction."[25] To enter into the intellectual history behind this resolution would be digressive, though only intellectual history can explain our learned societies' massive departures from common sense. I will very briefly mention the specific grammar instruction needed in the early grades to ensure that all students can master the conventions of the standard language.

Even children who have grown up speaking Standard American English in their homes find that certain discrepancies arise between written and oral forms. Given the massive stability and conservatism of the written language, it is very doubtful, as Henry Bradley pointed out, that the standard forms of written English will change during any time period we need be concerned with. The task of the schools is to adapt the student to the language, not vice versa. In the past, the teaching of grammar was a central feature of the common school (hence the nearly obsolete phrase "grammar school"). The curriculum was designed to familiarize students with the norms of formal written language. They had to diagram sentences to show they understood syntactical relationships. They had to know definitions of the parts of speech.

Grammar is not taught much anymore, with the result that estimable people self-consciously say things like "between he and I." The most unfortunate consequence of the schools' abandonment of grammar is that social mobility becomes ever more difficult for those students who did not grow up in educated homes, for whom the difference between oral and written language is great. The purpose of grammar instruction is to give students the ability to write and speak confidently in the public sphere without committing the errors that will cause other Americans to think of them as incompetent or not worth listening to. The example above is called "hypercorrection": the speaker wants to be very correct and therefore puts pronouns in the nominative case when they belong in the objective.

Educated under the anti-curriculum, antigrammar regime, an astonishing number of well-read and intelligent Americans make this mistake. They speak in this unnatural, self-conscious way because grammar has not been taught well—if at all. Nobody says "between he and I" in informal, un-self-conscious speech. It goes against the word-order principle of modern English to put a nominative at the end of a clause or sentence. In casual conversation, it's more natural to modern English to go just the other way.[26] People say and write solecisms like *between he and I* only because they are worried about making a mistake and because no one has properly taught them the very few points of grammar needed to avoid scorn.

To make students conversant with Standard English in early grades, the most important areas of grammar are subject-verb number agreement and pronoun case. The reason people make mistakes with pronouns is that standard American English is a word-order language, while the existing pronouns of Standard English are leftover vestiges from a time when English used word forms rather than word order to indicate word relationships. In modern English, "Dog bites man" means one thing, while "Man bites dog" means another, whereas in Old English (as in Latin) such relations could be shown by word form while keeping the word order more or less the same. We can still do this in modern English with pronouns, because they have different forms. "I hit him" is not the same as "Me he hit"—quite the contrary—though I/me comes first in both sentences.

Young students need to learn that *I* is the nominative, *me* the objective form, and that the nominative is the subject of a verb while the objective is the object of a verb or of a preposition such as *with*. Hence the correct form of "He went to the movies with John and ———" would be *with me*, never *with I*. If English had developed further before becoming fixed in writing, it might have used just one form—either *I* or *me*—for both nominative and objective case, and little would be lost. The same goes, of course, for *he* and *him, she* and *her, we* and *us, they* and *them,* and most confusing of all to many: *who* and *whom.* Since the accidents of history have left our immoveable standard language with these vestigial pronoun forms, from the long-past era when English was an inflected language, we sometimes have to pause in speech to decide which pronoun should be used where. It is a very simple matter to teach students how to do this so they will never forget it. It will be a great service to them if we do.

Of course, to know the difference between *I* and *me, she* and *her,* one has to know the difference between a subject and an object, so it is important to understand what phrases and clauses are and to know something about sentence structure. To impart such knowledge it is convenient to teach young students a vocabulary about language—such words as *subject* and *object, singular* and *plural, past, present,* and *future, sentence* and *clause,* as well as the parts of speech: *noun, verb, adjective, adverb, article, pronoun, conjunction, preposition.* American teachers are told that research shows such grammar instruction to be harmful or useless, but it is this spurious research that is questionable, not intelligent instruction in the grammar of the standard language. Teaching a few simple things about the parts of speech—not exclusively, not ad nauseam, not to the detriment of writing—is no more harmful than teaching the basic parts of plants. And for the child's future it is enormously more important.

5

Competence and Equality
Narrowing the Two Achievement Gaps

A few decades ago the United States had the most vibrant economy in the world. One reason given for our success was our educational system, then the most broadly based of any country's. Another was the willingness of American workers to move where the jobs were. Our famous worker mobility contributed to the flexibility and entrepreneurship of the economy as a whole. But the situation has changed. American workers can't move to China. Now there's an economic premium on a different kind of mobility—*intellectual* mobility, the skill of being able to learn new skills as the occasion demands. For most of the twentieth century and increasingly in the twenty-first, income level and general competence have been correlated with scores on a reading test.[1] Why should this be?

The Cause of the Two Achievement Gaps

It's because, in the information age, higher-paying jobs tend to be those that reward fast learning and good communication—all-purpose skills that depend on language mastery. Language mastery is not some abstract skill. It depends on possessing broad general knowledge shared by other competent people within the language community. Because our schools do not systematically impart this knowledge to all students, many American workers are ill equipped to adjust to new jobs. When they lose their old job, they are sunk. The theoretical advantages of free trade diminish for too many Americans when our poorly educated workers cannot in fact be trained for newer, better jobs. The theme of "retraining" as a consoling response to the job losses incurred by free trade is illusory if American workers cannot effectively be retrained.

American K-12 education has two fundamental shortcomings, one in achievement and the other in equity: the competence gap and the equality gap. The competence gap is shown in the OECD's assessment of student achievement in thirty countries, where we stand in the bottom quartile.[2] The equality gap is the large difference in reading achievement among demographic groups within the United States—wider than the gap between comparable groups in other nations with diverse populations.

The chief cause of the competence and equality gaps has been the anti-curriculum movement that took over in the United States during the latter half of the twentieth century. It cannot be emphasized too strongly, nor repeated too often, that the most important cause of our shortcomings is not laziness, unionism, waywardness, stupidity, or any moral fault among the leaders of our educational enterprise but rather a system of attractive but unsound ideas. The reigning intellectual monopoly has preserved the anti-curriculum ideology even in the face of its failures. Marxism, another failed system

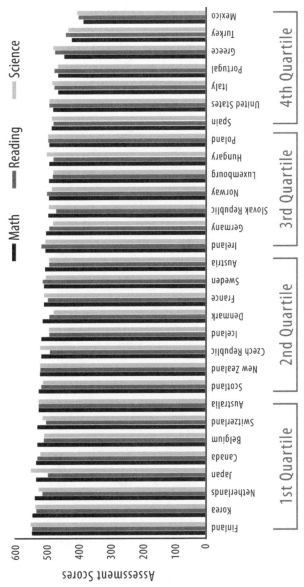

Scores of fifteen-year-olds in thirty countries, 2006. Source: OECD, Program for International Student Assessement.
Courtesy The Core Knowledge Foundation

of ideas, is readily blamed for the poor economic performance of the former Soviet Union, but the causal connections between anti-curriculum ideas and low academic achievement have not been widely identified or clearly understood. In this chapter I will examine more precisely why this well-intentioned ideology has depressed both competence and equality. At the same time, I will explain the positive evidence showing that an alternative set of ideas, built on what Carleton Washburne called "common essentials," can elevate the whole system and greatly narrow both gaps.

Before I offer this analysis, I will venture to arm the reader against two of the defenses that the education world has erected to explain away these gaps. The anti-curriculum movement originally claimed that an incidental, activities-based approach to learning would yield *superior* academic outcomes—more critical thinking, greater interest in school, deeper understanding, and other favorable results. Since the opposite has happened, the failure has been attributed not to the theory itself but to teachers' resistance to the theory. Even though anti-curriculum ideas have been triumphant for the better part of a century and realized in watered-down textbooks, it is claimed that teacher practices have not changed. The "new" ideas have never been properly tried in the schools. A whole scholarly industry has been devoted to this claim.[3] While the anti-curriculum theory insists that children ought to construct their own knowledge through their own activities, stubborn teachers, proponents argue, continue to lecture and drill their classes. Thus the theory has never truly been tried.[4] My counterargument is that the essence of the theory is not pedagogical method but the substitution of an activities-oriented, how-to curriculum for an academic curriculum. And that demonstrably *has* been tried on a large scale.

The "never tried" hypothesis might account for a lack of progress, but it cannot account for Americans' educational decline. That distressing development is explained away by a different defense—by denying that a genuine decline has occurred, despite our sinking international rankings and declining SAT scores. The main reason for the *apparent* decline, according to this defense, is that we now educate more poor and diverse students than ever before. Child poverty figures are cited, as well as the score discrepancies between whites and minorities. Attention is drawn to the (genuine) social inequities of our society to explain our educational inequities. Our educational system, this defense suggests, is really functioning pretty satisfactorily. It is just that we in the United States, unlike other countries, educate people who have long been in deep poverty. Our poor performance is the fault not of our schools but of the larger society.[5]

Though the word "poverty" is used in the self-exculpatory literature, it is usually a marker for "Hispanic" and "African American." In oral discussion, "poverty" is often a code word for "lower ability" and is connected with race and ethnicity. We are meant to assume that poverty is a less severe problem in other nations and that other nations educate a less diverse population—questionable assumptions. The anti-curriculum creed is thus protected by an implicit slur on the innate academic abilities of certain groups of low-income students. But this self-exculpation does not quite work. The gap in the reading tests of whites versus blacks and Hispanics is far greater than the gap in their IQ scores.[6] The explanation of the big achievement gap is not primarily genetic, social, or economic but educational.[7] It is far more likely that the decline of our schools is due to the decline of the academic curriculum. If we can demonstrate that poor black and Hispanic students of today make high scores when they attend a coherent, content-based school, then the poverty explanation fails. In science it is assumed that just a few counter-instances are quite enough to falsify a theory.

Karin Chenoweth, of the Education Trust, an organization devoted to disadvantaged students, has recently written a whole book of counter-instances, called *"It's Being Done."* This is what she says about the Capitol View School in Atlanta, 95 percent black, 3 percent Hispanic, and 88 percent poor:

> In stark contrast to schools that have "narrowed the curriculum" to focus on developing the skill of reading, Core Knowledge educators have broadened and deepened the curriculum to give students the background knowledge and vocabulary to read complex text. In the words of Trennis Harvey, the school's instruction specialist, "We teach reading through social studies and science." Reading is taught across the curriculum in several ways, from identifying antonyms and synonyms with science and social studies concepts, to reading fiction that matches the period the students are studying. "When we first started teaching reading through science and social studies four years ago," said principal Arlene Snowden, "it became really clear how excited and interested children were.

They are naturally curious about the world, and this way they learn about it."[8]

Chenoweth notes that Capitol View posted 100 percent grade-level proficiency ratings in reading, math, science, and social studies. Heartening examples beyond those in Chenoweth's book, and beyond Core Knowledge schools, can be easily supplied from non–Core Knowledge schools that follow a coherent curriculum. There are examples at every point of the socioeconomic spectrum.

Such results are not better known because the educational research community has simply not acknowledged their existence. Education professors apparently do not want to know about practical results that show that explicit, coherent subject matter counts for more than anything else in early education and produces results that far exceed anything done under the anti-curriculum creed. They have ignored Jeanne Chall's fine book *The Academic Achievement Challenge*. They do not research Core Knowledge schools. Professors have not encouraged their graduate students to pursue research into the effectiveness of content-based schools. Grant applications for big random-assignment studies of such schools have consistently been turned down by their review panels. Still, there is plenty of scientific and practical evidence available.[9]

Existing research shows that schools that teach common essentials increase competence and fairness simultaneously. A striking analysis done by Fred Smith in 2003 traced four well-matched cohorts in two well-matched schools through six grades of schooling. Here is what Smith found:

- Students who remained in the Core Knowledge school from kindergarten through sixth grade outperformed peers at the control school as measured by mean scaled scores on the Stanford 9 TA tests, which are standard grade-by-grade reading assessments used across the nation. Core Knowledge students outperformed control students in all subjects tested and for both of the two cohorts of students examined. The Core Knowledge advantage was statistically significant for reading ($p \leq .029$, $p \leq .002$) and math ($p \leq .002, p \leq .014$).

- Both advantaged and disadvantaged (free lunch) students in the Core Knowledge school outperformed students in the control school on the Stanford 9 TA tests. Again, this was true for all three subjects and for both cohorts examined. The disadvantaged students in the Core Knowledge school showed statistically significant advantages in reading ($p \leq .017$ for one cohort and $p \leq .030$ for the other). Core Knowledge thus promoted fairness in schooling by providing educational opportunity to disadvantaged as well as advantaged students.

- Core Knowledge helped narrow the achievement gap on the Stanford 9 TA test between advantaged and disadvantaged students. The achievement gap, as measured by the Stanford 9 TA tests, was narrowed for one Core Knowledge cohort and eliminated for the other. The achievement gap be-

tween advantaged and disadvantaged students remained large for both cohorts at the control school.

- Core Knowledge helped students achieve much
  larger gains on the Stanford 9TA tests over two-
  year periods, from fourth to sixth grades. Both advantaged and disadvantaged students made larger
  gains than their peers in the control school in all of
  the twelve cases evaluated. Among disadvantaged
  students, the edge to Core Knowledge was deemed
  highly significant in all three subjects ($p \leq .001$,
  $p \leq .001$ for reading; $p \leq .001$, $p \leq .001$ for math;
  $p \leq .001$, $p \leq .002$ for language).[10]

What Smith found was well supported by the scatter plot issued by the district of Albemarle County, Virginia, itself,
which showed the single Core Knowledge school in the district to be a significant outlier when student achievement was
plotted against income status.

The most plausible reason, then, for American academic
decline is not that the anti-curriculum theory has never been
properly tried or that poverty is to blame. It is that the anti-
curriculum theory is faulty, as predicted in the 1930s by Gramsci, Bagley, and Kandel, whose voices were drowned out. Cognitive science says that students will not learn what they have
not studied and that a direct approach to teaching and learning is more productive than an indirect, incidental approach.[11]
Common sense says much the same thing. One doesn't need
cognitive science to surmise that the low overall performance
of our schools might be caused by the incoherence and pau-

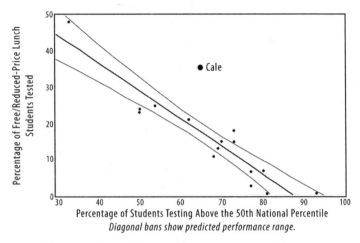

Diagonal bans show predicted performance range.

Albemarle County, Virginia, ITBS-1996 score performance
versus free/reduced-price lunch status. Courtesy
The Core Knowledge Foundation

city of the content being offered our students, especially in the
earliest grades.

Less obvious is why these shortcomings should dispro-
portionately affect disadvantaged students. In this chapter I
will describe how the competence gap and the equality gap are
interconnected. The very things we need to do to make a big
improvement in average student achievement will also greatly
narrow the equity gap between demographic groups. This exposition will briefly require me to go into some classroom detail. That is not a bad thing. What is missing from both free-
development theories and free-market theories of education is
that they do not explain with any specifics the mechanism by
which these grand schemes will yield greater prowess in math
or a bigger vocabulary.

The Correlation of Competence and Equality

A thesis of this book is that a *single* radical reform will go far to solving our three biggest educational problems—our decline in basic academic achievement, our failure to offer equality of educational opportunity, and our failure to perpetuate what Lincoln and others thought essential to the Union, a strong sense of loyalty to the national community and its civic institutions. All these shortcomings are amendable by intelligent attention to the specific common content of the early curriculum. It's perhaps obvious that greater commonality of knowledge will enhance a sense of national community. Less obvious is the necessary connection of common content with enhanced academic achievement and greater equality of opportunity.

It was the equality gap that first drew me into educational reform. I was doing experiments on reading and writing in the 1970s, first with students at the University of Virginia and then with students at a predominantly African-American community college in Richmond. I described the results in a technical publication of such obscurity that it is virtually unknown, but the results have colored all of my subsequent work in education.[12] What shocked me into school reform was the discovery that the African-American students at J. Sargeant Reynolds Community College in Richmond could read just as well as the University of Virginia students when the topic was roommates or car traffic, but they could not read passages about Robert E. Lee's surrender to Ulysses S. Grant. It was their performance on that particular text that shook me the most. They had graduated from the schools of Richmond, the erstwhile capital of the Confederacy, and were ignorant of the most elementary facts of the Civil War and other basic information normally taken for granted in the public sphere. They had not been taught the things they needed to know to understand texts addressed to a general audience. What had the schools been doing? I decided to switch careers and devote myself to helping right the wrong being done to these students.

When I started out in educational reform, there were already inklings of a correlation between school excellence and higher equity in the famous Coleman Report of 1966, called "Equality of Educational Opportunity." James Coleman and his colleagues showed that good schools had a greater positive effect on disadvantaged students than on advantaged ones, hence that really good schools are inherently compensatory. A school that achieves high scores for advantaged students will also narrow the fairness gap for disadvantaged students. By the same token, the Coleman Report showed that low-performing schools had a greater *negative* effect on disadvantaged students than on advantaged ones, thus supporting Gramsci's prediction of the 1930s that the anti-curriculum movement would increase social injustice.

So much emphasis was placed on another finding of Coleman's—that family background was more important than schools—that the critically important correlation between school quality and social equity has been widely overlooked. Moreover, the quality-equality correlation observed by Coleman and his colleagues reduces the force of their well-known finding about family background. If a school is academically good, its gap-narrowing potential *decreases* the importance of family background. Moreover, it must be remembered that the anti-curriculum movement was in full flower in the 1960s, ensuring that the general academic quality of American schools had already declined when Coleman was doing his research. This means that the relative effect of family background on educational performance had probably increased by the time Coleman and his team did their research.[13] Family background becomes relatively more important when schools fail to provide the knowledge that advantaged children gain in their homes.

African-American friends have told me that they directly experienced the recent decline of educational effectiveness for African-American students in American public schools. In the 1980s, one such friend spotted on my desk a grade-by-grade language-arts series from the 1920s called *Everyday Classics*. It was a wonderful series that had the announced double purpose of familiarizing students with the kinds of knowledge shared by other Americans and with the principles of the American experiment.[14] My friend nostalgically said that *those* were the textbooks she had studied in her segregated rural school in Virginia, and she regretted that her own children and nieces and nephews were getting nothing but pabulum in their bright new integrated schools. I have heard from other African Americans of my generation that the education blacks received in their Southern segregated schools was often better than the one their grandchildren are receiving now. This is one of the hidden facts about the post-*Brown* era that has kept integration from living up to its promise. Integration as such is far less critical to equality of educational opportunity than the quality of education actually received.

Recent international studies offer new support for Coleman's finding of a correlation between quality and equity in schooling. The OECD's assessment of students across thirty countries shows that the nations with the highest verbal scores are also the ones that have most effectively narrowed the equity gap between groups of students. The highest-achieving countries are Finland, Canada, Ireland, Japan, and Korea, and these are the very countries that show the least variation in eighth-grade student performance between advantaged and disadvantaged students.[15] The United States is in the middle in average verbal scores but low in equity.

International comparisons are unpersuasive to the majority of American educators, who say that other nations are not truly comparable to the United States—our apples are unlike their oranges. So let's look at individual states *within* the United States and let's not compare the states directly to each other, since that would lead to the same apples-oranges objection, but rather compare each state to itself by looking at its NAEP reading scores in 1998 and then in 2005 to see whether a rise in quality also produced a rise in equity.

Between 1998 and 2005, according to NAEP, only ten states showed any significant change in eighth-grade reading scores. Three states rose significantly: Delaware, Massachusetts, and Wyoming. The other seven—Arizona, Connecticut, New Mexico, Nevada, North Carolina, Rhode Island, and West Virginia—showed significant verbal decline. Let's see whether the states that *raised* average verbal scores also narrowed the gap between the 25th and the 75th percentiles of students. And let's also see whether states that declined increased the gap between the 25th and 75th percentiles. The answer is an emphatic yes to both questions.

A statistical analysis of the quality-equity nexus shows a

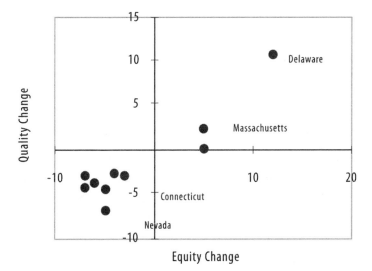

Quality change and equity change. Source: National Assessment
of Educational Progress. Courtesy The Core
Knowledge Foundation

0.92 correlation and a probability to the 0.0001 level—virtual
certainty—that the connection between a rise in quality and a
rise in equity is not random.

These are sensational results. Delaware, which started
from a very low point in 1998, showed the most gain in both
quality and equity, but the hero of the chart is Massachusetts,
which rose from the mid-top to the absolute top among the
states in average verbal score—without neglecting low-end
students. Massachusetts can of course do better on both met-
rics, as can all the states. But right now, if you are poor or black
or Hispanic and have a school-age child, the state to live in is
Massachusetts, where both the average reading scores and the
scores of the lower percentiles of students are higher than in

any other state. So Coleman's original finding of a connection between quality and equity is clearly visible among the OECD nations *and* among U.S. states. Why?

Explaining the Quality-Equality Nexus

It was to confirm the gap-narrowing effect of high academic quality that I searched the NAEP data to compare different states, and when the scatter plot showed a clear correlation, I was gratified but not surprised. When predictions are confirmed so strongly by archival data, it can have a bracing effect on one's confidence in a theory—especially when the confirmations are so powerful and unambiguous. Here's why I went looking for these correlations.

The work of Betty Hart and Todd Risley has demonstrated that toddlers in low-income homes tend to hear fewer words and less complex sentences than higher-income children. Low-income children therefore enter kindergarten or preschool with smaller verbal repertories than high-income children.[16] Keith Stanovich and his colleagues have shown why this early gap often increases with subsequent schooling. His term the "Matthew Effect" comes from the Gospel of Matthew: "For whosoever hath, to him shall be given, and he shall have more abundance: but whosoever hath not, from him shall be taken away even that he hath."[17]

Psycholinguistic studies explain why this Matthew Effect occurs.[18] One good way to understand it is in terms of vocabulary. The rich get richer in vocabulary and the poor get poorer because prior knowledge of key words enables advantaged children to learn still more new words from a discourse, whereas students who are ignorant of the verbal context are hindered in learning new words. Vocabulary researchers estimate, as a rough average, that a person needs to know about 90 percent of the words in a passage in order to make sense of it. The topic of vocabulary gain takes us to the pulsing heart of educational quality and equity. It shows why the rich get richer and the poor poorer, and how we can change that equation.

Let's picture a classroom where the more fortunate students know at least 90 percent of the words being used by a teacher or in a textbook. That enables them to gain knowledge about the other 10 percent of words that they did not already know. But the students who did not already know 90 percent of the words, and were therefore mystified by what the teacher or book said, would make little progress in learning new words and so would fall still further behind. They start off behind and then fall further behind. They also feel left out and discouraged and are likely to tune out and create discipline problems. For such students the verbal gap tends to grow ever larger as they go through school. The rich get richer and the poor get relatively poorer with exposure to the same discourse. That is the Matthew Effect.

But the NAEP scores show that this is not a completely accurate picture of what happens to disadvantaged students in the United States. The Matthew Effect predicts that the gap between demographic groups should grow larger as they move through the grades—the rich should continue to get richer and vice versa—but this does not happen. Rather, according to NAEP, the verbal gap starts out large and remains more or less the same from fourth through twelfth grade. In other words, our schools seem to be having no effect on fairness—which is a lot better than having a negative effect, as in Germany, Poland, and Luxembourg, where the gap grows larger in the higher grades. Our null result might have been predicted from our midpoint position on the OECD's quality-equity analysis. In the United States we do not do much to foster either quality or equity. On the other hand, it shows us that the Matthew Effect is not inevitable. Some entire national systems and, as we will see, some American schools have overcome it. How?

First we will need to make one small adjustment to the picture offered in the pathbreaking work of Hart and Risley and Stanovich. Their discussions are centered on language, but language is only part of the story in determining verbal scores. The family interactions with toddlers that Hart and Risley observed over many weeks and months were not just verbal. They were also referential—that is, the utterances referred to things and people in the world. If a toddler is told the difference between a wooden toy and a plastic toy, he or she not only learns the two words "wooden" and "plastic" but also gains knowledge about the world. Language is not a purely enclosed system. It is a tool we use to name, describe, and understand physical, social, and psychological realities. Advantaged children experience not only richer vocabularies and syntax but more of what that language refers to. This is implicitly understood by Hart, Risley, and Stanovich, but it is a point that needs to be amplified, because it holds the key to why some schools and some whole systems have been able to narrow the verbal gap.

Let's consider a real-life classroom to see how the gap narrowing occurs in high-quality schooling. Let's say a third-grade class is discussing farming and the Nile River. Here is a passage for children that I lifted from the Internet:

Farmers in ancient Egypt thought of the year as having three seasons: flood time, seeding, and harvest. Each year the Nile River would flood. This was good news for farmers because Egypt is mostly desert, and not enough rain falls to grow crops. The annual flood would last for a few weeks, and then the water level would drop, leaving a layer of fertile, black mud. This mud fertilized the soil, and the flood water was stored in a series of canals. A special government department was in charge of making sure the canals were kept in good repair.

Suppose that is read aloud to the students. Let's pretend that everyone in the class is already somewhat familiar with Egypt, with the Nile, and with farming, so that the passage makes some degree of sense to everybody in the class. This is a hugely important assumption about background knowledge that I will discuss in a moment. Let's also suppose that the *advantaged* children in the class also know a word that disadvantaged children do not know—the word "annual." But remember: all the students know enough about farming, Egypt, and the Nile to get the gist of the passage.

In this snapshot, we witness a tiny bit of gap narrowing. Why? Both advantaged and disadvantaged children begin to get a better handle on Egypt, farming, and the Nile. When they understand the gist of the discourse, all the children are able to make fairly accurate, if vague, guesses about the meanings of all the words. Hence disadvantaged students make gains in understanding "annual" that advantaged students do not make, because the advantaged students already knew that word. Disadvantaged children are learning even more from the passage than the advantaged ones. This illustrates the basic mechanism of gap narrowing at, so to speak, the molecular level. A little bit of catching up has occurred because those who started behind have learned a bit more about some words than those who already knew those words. The have-nots gained what the haves already had. This can be called the "anti-Matthew effect."

But notice how tiny the catching up was in this example and how very slow word learning is for all children, advantaged or disadvantaged. It takes many exposures to a word to gain a confident sense of its potential connotations. The slow cumulativeness of vocabulary growth cannot be overemphasized. Tiny changes build up gradually. It is widely stated that young children learn words at a remarkable rate—fifteen words a day—but that is not precisely what happens. Progress in verbal ability is a glacially slow process that occurs along a broad front. Children learn a tiny bit each day about hundreds of words, and what they learn in any given school year may be almost imperceptible. The accretive process takes place over several years.[19] The gains that occur in an individual class may be so small and so latent as to be unmeasurable. (No wonder short-term educational assessment is so hard!) It is only when a child reaches high school or college age and has acquired many thousands of words that researchers can divide that large total by the number of days the student has lived since age two. That is how they come up with the somewhat misleading number of fifteen words a day.

Once we understand this, we are in a position to explain the connection between fairness and quality in schooling. In the supportive environment of a good school, little dramas like the one about farming and the Nile and the word "annual" go on day after day. This process is the only underlying mechanism that has been proposed for narrowing the fairness gap in untracked classes. But this advance in equity can work only if the preconditions for comprehension are present for *all* children in the class. To understand the general sense of the Nile passage and guess the meanings of new words, students have to have been taught essential preparatory facts about Egypt and farming. They must already know that Egypt was a country in ancient times, that the year has seasons, that farming depends on planting seeds in moist soil, and that plants need nutrients and water to grow.

One cannot just assume that children have naturally absorbed this preparatory knowledge. One needs to take steps to ensure that they begin the lesson knowing some basic processes of farming and enough history and geography to make sense of the words "desert," "ancient Egypt" and "Nile." The ground for understanding that one Egypt lesson has to have been carefully prepared by a whole series of earlier lessons, some stretching back to previous years, to make the context adequately familiar to all the students in the class. Thus the only way to improve verbal scores for all children, advantaged and disadvantaged, is to prepare all of them for understanding classroom discourse by cumulatively building up the background knowledge they need to understand each day's classroom discourse. Without such long-range preparation, some of the students will remain mystified and the dread Matthew Effect will come into play.

That one lesson on Egypt is a microcosm of what schooling in general needs to do. It needs to provide students with the knowledge that will enable them to learn, understand, and communicate.

The benefits of coherent and cumulative knowledge preparation accrue to advantaged students as much as to disadvantaged ones. School time is being used productively. More is learned. Overall achievement is higher, the class moves forward rapidly, and the fairness gap is narrowed. Everyone in a classroom benefits if everyone has the background knowledge needed to understand the gist of classroom discourse. That, in a nutshell, is the basis for the quality-equity nexus. All students make gains, with disadvantaged children gaining relatively more because the groundwork has been carefully laid to make the classroom topic familiar to all. The late Harold Stevenson once observed, in his fine book with James Stigler called *The Learning Gap,* that the chief problem in American education is not diversity of income, race, and ethnicity but diversity of preparation. Ensuring that all students have the specific preparation they need to take the next step is the only route to higher quality and equity.

From our analysis of ancient Egypt and the Nile, readers will have perceived—or, I hope, at least be willing to entertain the idea—that this is the practical direction in which all of our schools need to go. The cumulative nature of growth in knowledge and language is the ground for my advocacy of an explicit core curriculum in the early grades. A carefully sequenced core curriculum is the only known way of ensuring that all the students in a classroom will be sufficiently familiar with the context of classroom discourse to be able to learn new words and ideas from it. If verbal skill involves knowledge of *things* as much as knowledge of language, then there is a need to teach knowledge of things systematically, cumulatively, and coherently. The more effectively we do that, the higher will be our students' achievement and the narrower will be the gaps between them.

With that understanding, we are in a position to see why Finland and Massachusetts score so well on the equity-quality metric. Finland has instituted a specific core curriculum that comprises about 60 percent of the whole curriculum, leaving the other 40 percent to the localities. School tests are based on this core curriculum. And of all the states in the nation, Massachusetts has come closest to that pattern. It has fairly specific knowledge guidelines and has instituted challenging tests—the MCAS (Massachusetts Comprehensive Assessment System)—that genuinely follow the guidelines. There is much room for improvement in these guidelines and tests, but their basic structure and the seriousness with which that structure has been realized over the past decade have brought Massachusetts to the top in both quality and fairness.

Schools That Narrow the Two Gaps

Looking for a school for your child? What about this one?

The Ridgeview Classical School in Fort Collins has been rated among the top three schools in Colorado since it was founded in 2001. Its success stands as a sharp rebuke to the dominant anti-intellectual pedagogy of most American schools. The secret of its success? The Core Knowledge curriculum in Kindergarten through 8th grade, and a traditional, Classical-Liberal curriculum in high school. An article in the Grand Junction Sentinel highlights the school and its remarkable achievements.

"They have phenomenal success," said Denise Mund, senior consultant with Schools of Choice at the Colorado Department of Education. "Their school for years was the No. 1 school in the state. This year, they were third, but repeatedly, they have had phenomenal success."

Alfie Kohn and others who have dismissed Core Knowledge as "rote memorization" should heed the teacher at Ridgeview who says of Core Knowledge, "It's just dynamic. The core curriculum has changed the way that I teach. It is set up on a sequence of things that should be learned and starts at rudimentary levels in kindergarten, first and second grade. I think it's history-based, and music and art are right in the curriculum. It's all put together in a very sequential plan."[20]

A school in Roxbury, Massachusetts, Roxbury Preparatory Charter School, is experiencing similarly outstanding success with poor minority students. It has "200 students of color, 68 percent of whom qualify for the federal free and reduced price lunch program."[21] It is not a Core Knowledge school. Its success is explained by its having created, completely on its own, a curriculum comparable in explicitness to the Core Knowledge sequence. The school's energetic and devoted staff started with the relatively detailed grade-level content standards published by Massachusetts (recognizing their variable quality in the different subjects) and then gathered all the past state grade-level tests in the various subjects. From these materials, Roxbury created day-by-day content standards for grades six to eight. The resulting curriculum is set forth with great specificity and detail. Here is how it is described on the school's web site:

> Though not every Roxbury Prep standard corresponds directly with the Massachusetts state standards, every Massachusetts standard is addressed and receives significant attention in the Roxbury Prep curriculum. Using Roxbury Prep's Curriculum Alignment Template (CAT), teachers ensure that every Massachusetts and Roxbury Prep standard is addressed with a class lesson and that every class lesson addresses at least one standard. Roxbury Prep teachers distribute the academic standards and weekly syllabi to students and families. Syllabi include daily objectives, activities, and homework assignments.[22]

As a result, the school's predominantly poor, African-American student body has more than closed the equity gap:

> The percentage of Roxbury Prep students scoring Advanced or Proficient was higher than that of the state's White students. Roxbury Prep demonstrates with clarity that the long-standing "racial achievement gap" can be closed. On the 8th grade math test, Roxbury Prep had the highest percentage of students

scoring Advanced or Proficient (94%) of any school in Massachusetts. Roxbury Prep students scored Advanced or Proficient at a higher rate than students in Wayland (82%), Wellesley (74%), and Weston (74%). Moreover, Roxbury Prep students outperformed students attending the prestigious Boston Latin School (90%).

Better than Boston Latin! But you do not have to be a charter school to accomplish this sort of thing. Plenty of regular public schools are Core Knowledge schools. They first had to be brave enough to resist the hostility to the idea of a set curriculum, and they have in fact managed to raise achievement levels and greatly narrow the gap between demographic groups. In 2007, the Department of Education issued a report called *K-8 Charter Schools: Closing the Achievement Gap,* featuring seven schools from seven geographical regions, two of which were Core Knowledge schools. That these were charter schools, however, is not the relevant fact: the key was the teachers and the curriculum. As Karin Chenoweth has shown in *"It's Being Done,"* we find the same gap-narrowing effects in unheralded Core Knowledge public schools all over the nation.

Over time, implementing a coherent set curriculum does more than raise achievement for all; after six or seven years it nearly erases the gap between demographic groups. That is exactly what researchers discovered in France, where early preschool is followed by a coherent curriculum in elementary school. Nationwide, in France, the demographic gap almost disappears by the end of sixth grade.[23] These are large-scale results, not isolated instances of closing the equality gap.

One of the best schools in New York City is the Carl Icahn School, a very low-income, largely black and Latino, Core Knowledge school that well outscores its high-income neighbors. It is being run by Jeffrey Litt, an energetic, independent-minded principal who in the early 1990s started an earlier Core Knowledge school, the second to come into existence. New York City keeps excellent records these days and has noticed that the highest quality-equity scores in the city are found in a handful of Core Knowledge schools. (One enterprising New York superintendent, Kathleen Kashin, has created a support organization to begin implementing the curriculum in some one hundred public schools.)

Here is an interesting chart from the 2007 report of verbal scores in New York City charter schools, issued by the New York State Department of Education. It gives the average percentages of students who read at the proficient or advanced levels. It is informative to compare the figures for the two Core Knowledge (CK) charter schools with those of the host district and the three KIPP (Knowledge Is Power Program) charter schools. KIPP schools are known as wonderful middle schools emphasizing discipline and hard work and more hours on academics that have received a lot of financial help and publicity from proponents of charter schools. They have shown remarkable results in math and good results in reading. But as the foregoing analysis would suggest, middle school is rather late to begin intensive work in language.

All schools in this chart have similar demographics: nearly 100 percent disadvantaged students. The proficiency numbers shown here stand for percentages of students who are reading at grade level.

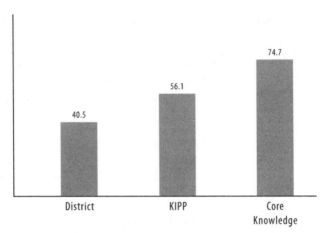

Fifth-grade reading proficiency in New York City.
Source: New York State Department of Education.
Courtesy The Core Knowledge Foundation

To be fair, the fifth-grade students in the KIPP schools
were in their school just one year, whereas some of the CK students had been in their school for several years. But that, after
all, is the point. The *cumulative* effect of a coherent curriculum is what ultimately makes the difference. Knowledge of language and knowledge of things needs to be fostered productively from the earliest grades. These all-important verbal
scores are not highly amenable to short-term intensive work in
middle and high school. The much-admired KIPP schools
would be even better if they started in the early grades and
adopted a cumulative, year-by-year core curriculum set up in
advance.

In this chapter I have dealt with the nitty-gritty foundations of fairness and high achievement in the critical early
grades. The positive implications for America's economic and

civic future are significant. I have offered specific examples of schools that disconfirm the poverty theory of low achievement and other self-exculpations of the educational establishment. Each of these schools has narrowed both gaps by putting the pro-curriculum theory into practice. There are no comparable examples of gap narrowing by schools that use the methods of the anti-curriculum theory. There could not be. There is simply no known mechanism of learning that would enable the dominant American educational theory of the past century to achieve such a positive result.

6

Competence and Community
Renewing Public Education

In the last chapter I noted that scores on fill-in-the-bubble reading tests are the most reliable predictors of Americans' future economic status and ability to become effective citizens.[1] Reading is an act of communication with complete strangers who share the public sphere. Reading ability embraces the multiple skills one needs in order to become effective in that sphere, including a readiness to write and speak well.[2] It is a special kind of communication that necessarily makes use of a large dimension of unwritten knowledge required to understand what an absent stranger is trying to convey by words coming from a loudspeaker, printed on a page, or reproduced on a computer screen.

From the ability to understand strangers and make oneself understood in turn, other competencies flow. One can learn new things readily, prosper in school, and possess the general knowledge needed to train for a new job. No Child Left Behind reasonably places a big emphasis on reading tests, but that has unfortunately accounted for the unintended consequence that much time is being misspent on how-to skills and test preparation. Stagnant, even declining twelfth-grade scores on reading tests indicate that our schools do not fully understand what they must do to help students achieve high scores on these tests. I therefore begin this final chapter with a brief analysis of what is required (beyond the mechanical aspects of reading—decoding skill and fluency) to make a high score on these tests. I make the following guarantee: any state or district that follows the principles outlined here will raise its reading scores (and therefore the competencies of its students) to a high international level.

How to Ace a Reading Test

Reading tests are attacked for cultural bias and other faults, but such complaints are unfounded. The tests are fast and accurate indexes of real-world reading ability. They correlate extremely well with one another and with actual capacity to learn and communicate.[3] They consist, after all, of written passages, which students are to read and then answer questions on; that is, students are asked to exercise the very skill at issue. The rhetorical campaign against these tests relies heavily on the term "standardized." Most people think the word refers to a soulless, fill-in-the-bubble format, but the term actually means that scoring conditions have been regularized so that any version of the test given on any occasion will yield approximately the same score for students of similar reading abilities. Standardized tests are thus fair. The complaints would be even more vigorous if the tests were *un*-standardized and therefore unfair. Administering a reading test takes relatively little time out of the school year. The much more reasonable complaint is that an emphasis on testing has caused schools to devote too much time to drills and test preparation, with a consequent narrowing of the curriculum.

That is true. Linda Perlstein has documented how the enforced practice of formal techniques conducted on vapid readings has displaced time that young children could and should spend on history, science, and the arts.[4] Yet the fault lies not with the tests but with the school administrators who have been persuaded that it is possible to drill for a reading test—on the mistaken assumption that reading is a skill like typing and that once you know the right techniques you can read any text addressed to a general audience. The bulk of time in early language-arts programs today is spent practicing these abstract strategies on an incoherent array of uninformative fictions. The opportunity costs have been enormous. Schools are wasting hours upon hours practicing drills that are supposed to improve reading but that are actually depriving students of knowledge that could enhance their reading comprehension. Ever since this cramming has been put into effect, reading scores in later grades have trended downward, because the cramming has driven out the very thing—coherent content—that could enable children to ace their reading tests. To explain this paradox, let's look at some actual tests children must take.

Here is the beginning of an actual passage from a New York State reading test for fourth grade:

There is a path that starts in Maine and ends in Georgia, 2,167 miles later. This path is called the Appalachian Trail. If you want, you can walk the whole way, although only some people who try to do this actually make it, because it is so far, and they get tired. The idea for the trail came from a man named Benton Mac-Kaye. In 1921 he wrote an article about how people needed a nearby place where they could enjoy nature and take a break from work. He thought the Appalachian Mountains would be perfect for this.

The passage goes on for a while, and then come the questions. The first question, as usual, concerns the main idea:

This article is mostly about
1. how the Appalachian Trail came to exist.
2. when people can visit the Appalachian Trail.
3. who hikes the most on the Appalachian Trail.
4. why people work together on the Appalachian Trail.

Many educators see this question as probing the general skill of "finding the main idea." It does not. Try to put yourself in the position of a disadvantaged fourth grader who knows nothing of hiking, does not know the difference between an Appalachian-type mountain and a Himalayan-type mountain, does not know where Maine and Georgia are, and does not grasp what it means to "enjoy nature." Such a child, though much trained in comprehension strategies, might answer the question incorrectly. The student's more advantaged counterpart, not innately smarter, just happens to be familiar with hiking in the Appalachians, has been to Maine and Georgia, and has had a lot of experience "enjoying nature." The second student easily answers the various questions correctly. But not because he or she practiced comprehension strategies; this student has the background knowledge to comprehend what the passage is saying.

Teachers and administrators are told that students' scores will improve on such tests if they are compelled to practice strategies like questioning the author and finding the main idea. But the research foundations for this claim are questionable, especially if one factors in opportunity cost—what schools could be doing during the same time periods that would improve reading even more.[5] This oversight is only partly the fault of the schools: they are following the recommendations of the *Report of the National Reading Panel,* which is weak and unreliable in its section on reading comprehension.[6]

It has been shown decisively that subject-matter knowledge trumps formal skill in reading and that proficiency in one reading-comprehension task does not necessarily predict skill in another.[7] Test makers implicitly acknowledge this by offering, in a typical reading test, as many as ten passages on varied topics. (If reading were a knowledge-independent skill, a single passage would suffice.) Operating under the how-to conception of reading, the schools find themselves in a Kafkaesque situation in relation to reading tests. Like Josef K in *The Trial,* teachers and students are dutifully trying to obey all the instructions by practicing the time-consuming strategy exercises demanded by the authorities, but they have still not managed to fulfill the mysterious requirements of the test. The key conceptual mistake is that, contrary to appearances and educators' beliefs, these reading tests do not test comprehension *strategies.*

There are usually questions like "What is the main idea of this passage?" but such a question probes ad hoc comprehension, not some general technique of finding the main idea. Reading comprehension is not a universal, repeatable skill like sounding out words or throwing a ball through a hoop. "Reading skill" is rather an overgeneralized abstraction that obscures what reading really is: an array of separate, content-constituted skills such as the ability to read about the Appalachian Mountains or the ability to read about the Civil War.

The specific knowledge dependence of reading tests becomes obvious in those given in the later grades. Here is a passage from a tenth-grade Florida state test:

> The origin of cotton is something of a mystery. There is evidence that people in India and Central and South America domesticated separate species of the plant thousands of years ago. Archaeologists have discovered fragments of cotton cloth more than 4,000 years old in coastal Peru and at Mohenjo Daro in the Indus Valley. By A.D. 1500, cotton had spread across the warmer regions of the Americas, Eurasia, and Africa. Today cotton is the world's major nonfood crop, providing half of all textiles. In 1992, 80 countries produced a total of 83 million bales, or almost 40 billion pounds. The business revenue generated—some 50 billion dollars in the United States alone—is greater than that of any other field crop. Most of the five billion pounds that U.S. mills spin and weave into fabric each year ends up as clothing.

It would take many pages to indicate even a significant fraction of the tacit knowledge needed to understand this passage. The main subject, cotton, is not defined. You must already know what it is, a reasonable assumption. It also helps to have an idea of how it grows and how it is harvested and then put into bales. (What's a bale?) Then consider the throwaway statement that different people "domesticated separate species of the plant thousands of years ago." To domesticate a species of a plant is not an action that is self-evident from everyday knowledge. Ask a group of tenth graders what it means to domesticate a plant, and chances are that most will not know. Of course, they *should* know. Domestication of plants is fundamental to human history. But most do not, and they will not understand that part of the test passage no matter how well they can perform other tasks currently taught in language-arts classes. The writer of this passage (which was, the state of Florida informs us, taken from *National Geographic*) clearly expected his readers to know what cotton is and what plant domestication is. He expected them to know that the Indus Valley is many thousands of miles from Peru. (How many tenth graders know *that?*)

This passage illustrates the way reading comprehension works in the real world of magazines, training manuals, textbooks, newspapers, web sites, and books. The writer assumes that readers know some things but not others. In this case, readers were expected to know some geography and history and something about agriculture but not how long human beings have used cotton—the new information supplied in the passage. That is exactly how a school textbook or the Internet offers new information: it is embedded in a mountain of taken-for-granted knowledge. That is the way language *always* works.

I was once invited by *Education Week,* an influential journal in the school world, to write a short piece giving my reasons for asserting that, beyond a few short lessons, the teaching of reading-comprehension strategies is a waste of time. I hit on the idea of presenting a mock reading test containing a passage chosen completely at random from one of the most influential books ever written—Immanuel Kant's notoriously difficult *Critique of Pure Reason.* The passage went like this:

> A manifold, contained in an intuition which I call mine, is represented, by means of the synthesis of understanding, as belonging to the necessary unity of self-consciousness, and this is effected by means of the category. This requirement of a category therefore shows that the empirical consciousness of a given manifold in a single intuition is subject to a pure self-consciousness a priori, just as is empirical intuition to a pure sensible intuition, which likewise takes place a priori.

I asked educators to pretend they were in the position of students taking a reading test and were being asked a typical multiple-choice question:

The main idea of this passage is
 1. without a manifold, one cannot call an intuition "mine."
 2. intuition must precede understanding.

3. intuition must occur through a category.
4. self-consciousness is necessary to understanding.

I offered the readers of *Education Week* lots of time to apply the strategies they compel children to practice: summarize, classify, and find the main idea. If that didn't help, they might try the strategy of "questioning the author": What is Kant trying to get at here? Most, I suspect, were still clueless.

But if you had been taught about the problem Kant was trying to solve and how he attempted to solve it, you could correctly guess that the right answer is 3. To get the right answers on a reading test takes what cognitive psychologists call "domain-specific knowledge," a principle that holds for all language communication. The point of my essay was that it is far more fruitful to teach children the broad array of domain-specific knowledge they will need to become mature readers than to practice reading strategies such as "finding the main idea," "clarifying," and "summarizing." The vast amounts of time teachers and students currently spend on those strategy exercises is time they are not spending on domains of knowledge that are critical for understanding books, newspapers, newscasts, and the great grab bag of information that is the Internet. In subsequent letters to the editor, the response of the anti-curriculum establishment was the usual ad hominem dismissal: Pay no attention to Hirsch. He is only trying to make money from his Core Knowledge books.

A reading test is inherently a knowledge test. Scoring well requires familiarity with the subjects of the test passages. Hence the tests are unfair to students who, through no fault of their own, have little general knowledge. Their homes have not provided it, and neither have the schools. This difference in knowledge, not any difference in ability, is the fundamental reason for the reading gap between white and minority students. We go to school for many years partly because it takes so long to build up the vast general knowledge and vocabulary we need to become mature readers.

Because this knowledge-gaining process is slow and cumulative, the type of general reading test now in use could be fair to all groups only above fifth or sixth grade, and only after good, coherent, content-based schooling in the previous grades. I therefore propose a policy change that would at one stroke raise reading scores and narrow the fairness gap. (As a side benefit, it would induce elementary schools to impart the general knowledge children need.) Let us institute curriculum-based reading tests in first, second, third, and fourth grades—that is to say, reading tests containing passages based on knowledge that children will have received directly from their schooling. In the early grades, when children are still gaining this knowledge slowly and in piecemeal fashion, it is impossible to give a fair reading test of any other sort.[8]

To carry out this idea, the education department of a state will need to announce something like the following: "Here is the specific core curriculum that students should learn in the first five grades. For the next five years our reading tests for each grade will contain passages from domains taken from that coherent curriculum: such as Greek and Roman myths, *Alice in Wonderland*, 'Ali Baba and the Forty Thieves,' 'The People Who Could Fly,' the geography of the Mediterranean Sea, Julius Caesar, the Hopi and Zuni Indians, Ponce de León and

Florida, Canada, the Thirteen Colonies before the Revolution, the families of musical instruments, the speed of light, sound and the human ear, and the solar system."[9] At the same time that the state made this announcement it would also make available the materials and professional guidance teachers would need to teach those topics effectively. Because more topics would be listed than would be tested, *all* the topics the state mentioned would likely be taught. Tests would continue to drive schooling—as always—but they would do so in an educationally productive way that systematically enhanced background knowledge. Offering children a good education is the right way to cram for a reading test.

We now have an answer to our question of how to enable all children to ace a reading test. We need to impart systematically—starting in the very earliest grades by reading aloud to students, then later in sequenced self-reading—the general knowledge that is taken for granted in writing addressed to a general audience. If reading tests in early grades are based on a universe of pre-announced topics, general knowledge will assuredly be built up. By later grades, when the reading tests become the standard non-curriculum one, such as the NAEP tests, reading prowess will have risen dramatically.[10]

Policy makers say they want to raise reading scores and narrow the fairness gap. But it seems doubtful that any state can now resist the anti-curriculum outcry that would result from actually putting curriculum-based testing into effect. Nonetheless, any state or district that courageously instituted knowledge- and curriculum-based early reading tests would see a very significant rise in students' reading scores in later grades.

Why the Early Grades Are Far More Critical than High School

The Bill and Melinda Gates Foundation has given hundreds of millions of dollars for high school reform—with disappointing results. For many years, the philanthropic and policy worlds have emphasized the two ends of precollegiate education— high school and preschool. They are right about preschool but not about high school. The general knowledge and vocabulary required for effective learning at the high school level are slow-growing fruits of a long process. The way to reform high school is to prepare elementary school students to thrive there. If, over time, high school has become a smorgasbord of watered-down subjects, it is because watered-down subjects are all most students are now prepared to understand.

Most people accept that high school is a place to study actual subjects like chemistry and American history. The victory of the anti-curriculum movement has chiefly occurred in the crucial early grades, and the further down one goes in the grades, the more intense is the resistance to academic subject matter, with the greatest wrath reserved for introducing academic knowledge in preschool. It does not seem to occur to the intellectual descendents of Rousseau that the four-year-old children of rich, highly educated parents might be gaining academic knowledge at home that is unfairly being withheld at school (albeit with noble intentions) from the children of the poor.

In recent years, the debate over academics in educational reform has concerned itself with the later grades. The most influential educational document of recent years, *A Nation at*

Risk (1983), focused on high school; there had been a severe decline in verbal and math scores in high school, which was considered the truly decisive arena for educational improvement. For most of its length, *A Nation at Risk* ignored the first eight grades of schooling, its assumption being that those years are foundational and should be spent absorbing the enabling skills of reading, writing, and reckoning. Then, in its last pages, the report finally mentioned the early curriculum: "The curriculum in the crucial eight grades leading to the high school years should be specifically designed to provide a sound base for study in those and later years in such areas as English language development and writing, computational and problem solving skills, science, social studies, foreign language, and the arts. These years should foster an enthusiasm for learning and the development of the individual's gifts and talents."[11]

It was natural for the commissioners to seek reform where the most notable declines seemed to appear—and this emphasis on later grades was reinforced by the observation that the declines were accompanied by ever more fragmented high school curricula. But in the longer historical perspective, the watering down of high school was less a cause of lower scores than a consequence of the gradual decline of learning. In re-reading *A Nation at Risk* I was reminded of a repairman who once came to fix a leak in our washing machine. He asked my wife where the leak was, and she said, "At the bottom." He responded, "Yeah, that's what they all say."

The authors of *A Nation at Risk* accepted the how-to view of early education that now dominates the American educational world. They assumed that any sensible content will do so long as it develops the necessary foundational skills. One cannot fault them for this. How could they think otherwise when there was unanimity among experts? Here is how they described a hearing entitled "Language and Literacy," held in April 1982:

> A panel of five Commission members . . . heard testimony regarding the development of the higher-order language skills necessary for academic learning. Six invited speakers presented national perspectives on teaching reading, writing, and second languages, and discussed related concerns with the Commission members. Sixteen other speakers presented their views on the hearing topics, predominantly from regional and local perspectives. The general theme provided by the witnesses was that the language skills that should be emphasized were the more sophisticated, integrated, concept-oriented skills of comprehension and composition.[12]

Throughout their report, the commissioners implied that the battle for educational improvement in early grades would be won when students went beyond the basics and mastered "higher-order skills." As a consequence, neither they nor their witnesses said anything about the actual content of early schooling. The path to improvement is the early grades was seen to lie less in the substance that was taught than in developing higher-order proficiencies.

Decades later, elementary schools continue to follow the advice of the anti-curriculum experts to impart higher-order skills such as "critical thinking" and "problem solving." Yet according to international studies, these skills turn out to be precisely the ones our students lack compared with students in Asian and European countries that place less emphasis on formal skills and more on coherent year-to-year subject matter.[13] Higher-order skills are important, but they are not learned best by endlessly focusing on them. If you are reading these words, you undoubtedly possess the skills advocated by *A Nation at Risk*—you can read my words with comprehension and think about them critically. Somehow you and I gained these skills without being taught them directly.

How did we manage this? Cognitive science is clear: through domain-specific knowledge and through practice. By the time *A Nation at Risk* was published in 1983, cognitive psychology had achieved a consensus about the knowledge-based character of most school-based skills and the importance of long practice. But cognitive psychology was not often alluded to in *A Nation at Risk,* and today there is still little crossover between cognitive science and educational policy. *A Nation at Risk* simply assumed that gaining an academic skill such as reading or reckoning is independent of the specific curricular content through which the skill is taught. This is wrong.[14]

In his superb book *The Number Sense,* Stanislas Dehaene makes an observation about mathematical expertise that has general application to most higher-order skills. He asked how it is that some people who are only modestly above average in basic math abilities can after a time perform astonishing feats of mathematical insight and mental calculation—far beyond what ordinary people can achieve. The key, it turns out, is the phrase "after a time." Mathematicians and mental calculators are made, not born. They begin with a small basic advantage in math ability that leads them to take pleasure in math. Doing problems and practicing calculations is a rewarding activity for them, and they practice math more and more. Those of us who lack that small initial edge take less pleasure in the activity, study less, and practice less.[15]

What makes a math genius is thus similar to what makes a great musical performer: a small advantage in talent that leads, with years of effort and study, to a big advantage in achievement—as in the old joke "How do you get to Carnegie Hall?" Answer: "Practice, practice, practice." In general, it is not some Superman-like endowment that accounts for high expertise in any subject but rather tenacity of practice (lasting, on average, some ten years).[16] What is true of math and music is also true of language. Wide knowledge and a large vocabulary—the prerequisites to achievement in high school—are gradual accretions. You cannot gain them by a sudden intensive incursion in the later grades. With a slow, tenacious buildup of knowledge and vocabulary in elementary school, high school will almost take care of itself.

An American Core Curriculum for Early Grades

The policy implications of this book can be boiled down to this: Institute in your district or state an explicit, grade-by-grade, core curriculum in grades K-8 occupying at least 50 percent of school time. Because a nationwide core curriculum is not in the offing, the best policy for now is for each state to institute a good elementary core curriculum, either on its own or in cooperation with other states, and to assume that a desirable tendency toward ever greater commonality among the states will emerge over time. There are no good educational arguments against a coherent, content-specific core curriculum that could possibly outweigh the many good reasons for its superior efficacy and fairness. Nevertheless, prejudices against commonality, and indeed against any set curriculum, continue to dominate American education. In the next section I will discuss these inert prejudices, which still constitute perhaps our biggest barrier to educational improvement. But first it will be useful to discuss how we might actually create a common content core—if a state or district decided it was a good idea to do so.

First, how would we answer the conversation stopper "Who will decide?"? The gotcha implication of this question is the assumption that no group can legitimately arrogate to itself the power to determine a common core of content for a whole state or nation—especially not in a multiplex society like ours. But this is a rhetorical ploy, not an argument. The problem has been solved in other multicultural liberal democracies. In fact no high-performing and fair educational system has failed to solve it. If an American core curriculum can meet two criteria—*acceptability* and *effectiveness*—then the political problem can be solved, and there will be a real chance to reverse decades of American educational decline.[17]

Acceptability: We know from surveys that the public generally likes the idea of a common core and wants the schools to teach the traditions that hold the country together—traditions such as respect for those laws, institutions, and ideals of freedom and equality that Abraham Lincoln exhorted American schools to promote in order to preserve the union as the "last best hope of earth." Lincoln's view is seconded by most citizens. In the Public Agenda report *A Lot to Be Thankful For,* 84 percent of parents said they wanted their children to learn about America's political institutions, history, and ideals of freedom and equality. Concerning civics, then, the America public has clearly decided the core-curriculum question. Moreover, few sensible people will wish to launch a campaign against a core curriculum in math and science, which are the same in China as in Chattanooga. But there is a lot more to elementary education than civics, math, and science. We also need agreement on a common core for history, art, music, and literature—a more daunting task that leads to the second characteristic a common core must exhibit: effectiveness.

Effectiveness: An explicit curriculum would be accepted in the United States if it were shown to be highly effective in imparting an ability to read, write, and learn at a high level. Effectiveness and acceptability go together in the public mind—especially in the early grades, where the ability to comprehend the written and spoken word is tied up with the shared background knowledge already tacitly accepted by the community. I began the Core Knowledge project several decades ago when I came to realize that an effective core curriculum in the early grades would be one that imparted this community-based knowledge. Hence the answer to the question "Who decides?" is "The language community has already largely decided." Any impulse to change the character of the community's shared knowledge should be a matter of open, vigorous, democratic debate, not something imposed by ideologues on the poor. That communally shared knowledge can be inventoried and taught to children. A core curriculum that systematically imparts this content will be optimally effective in developing reading, writing, and learning ability. This technical insight is the heart of the Core Knowledge movement and explains its effectiveness in raising reading and writing scores. Americans are pragmatists. Effectiveness of schooling is the criterion that will count most with the public. Effectiveness is the key to acceptability. This book is not an advertisement for Core Knowledge but for the scientifically sound principles on which it has been formed.

Anyone interested in developing a curriculum on such principles might look at the introduction to *The Core Knowledge Sequence,* where my colleagues and I describe how we created it.[18] We first got some agreement on the tacitly shared knowledge young people need to possess to become good readers, writers, and learners in present-day America. Once that compendium had been developed, we sought to determine if experienced teachers would reach some agreement about an intelligent sequencing of that knowledge in a school curriculum. From the input of teachers around the country we created a draft sequence for grades K-6, which we distributed for comment. Then, in 1990, we held a working conference. Some 120 people, representing different organizations and interest groups, who had been sent the draft sequence in advance, met in Charlottesville, Virginia, for several days to amend this document. Each table of eight people (with changing membership for each session) held morning and afternoon sessions on a specific part of the sequence. At the end of each day we reported out to a plenary session and voted.

Despite the intensity of identity politics in the 1980s and 1990s, a mundane practical principle enabled this diverse group of people to reach agreement on a definite core. The principle was this: if a group agreed to add something to a grade level, they also had to agree to take something out. If a topic was switched to a different grade level, other adjustments had to be made for integration and coherence.[19] These practical restrictions imposed a useful discipline that made us keep in view the practicalities of teaching what is most needed to understand the written word in the American public sphere. By the time the various groups reported out in plenary sessions, the participants, who had started out full of mutual suspicion, ended up a band of brothers and sisters—having done something that was clearly animated by the desire to benefit students and the community as a whole. We were all aware that in the *other* 50 percent of the curriculum, the unspecified half, teachers, schools, and localities could express very different preferences.

The result was multicultural as well as traditional and was acceptable to all the groups involved. We wanted a distinctively American core but were aware how arbitrary some of the specific decisions had to be. It is a grave intellectual error to make too much of this arbitrariness, just as it would be to complain of the decision to drive on the right side of the road rather than the left. Decisions must be made. Any reasonable ones can sustain the language community. All modern national knowledge assumptions are arbitrarily invented constructs— put together with glue and thread, as scholars like Ernest Gellner and Eric Hobsbawm have shown. Over time these arbitrary constructs become traditional. (Hobsbawm's book on the subject is called *The Invention of Tradition*.)[20] Once shared knowledge assumptions have been in place for a time in books and schools, they become, like the standard language, a system that is difficult to change except at the edges. The early curriculum should emphasize the most stable dimensions of the language community's shared traditions, as recorded in the books of its libraries. At the same time, in the United States, that agreed-on core should gradually come to reflect consensus changes toward greater inclusiveness and progress in social justice, which are part of our founding ideal.

There are numerous ways of combining effectiveness with acceptability in developing a core curriculum, but the general principles we followed in 1990 should be helpful to anyone attempting to do the same. Any effective core for American schools will implicitly follow some of the same principles, because the knowledge that is most needed for high literacy in the United States is fairly stable. There is a definite body of knowledge taken for granted in the language community.[21] To show concretely why this is so, I reproduce in appendix 1 the history and geography thread of the Core Knowledge Sequence from kindergarten through second grade. Such a full example is needed to give an adequate idea of the cumulative effect of a genuine curriculum, though, of course, the reader need not pore over the details. These three grades' worth of history and geography—all well field-tested—show how knowledgeable and ready to learn students will have become by the end of only the second grade.

What We Are Up Against

In this section I will illustrate some of the difficulties that will beset those who attempt to institute a core curriculum in their schools. Some of the illustrations are taken from my experience—I happen to be a good source of experiences on this score—but the point is not my frustration. Rather, I aim to show the sort of thing that future curriculum reformers will need to prepare themselves for. Reformers will not need to sharpen their scientific wits so much as their rhetorical ones. No one has produced a scientifically acceptable argument against commonality in a core curriculum. For example, it is not difficult to refute the claim that "cookie-cutter" sameness causes everyone to think alike. One need only point to fierce disagreements in core-curriculum countries like France and Finland, not to mention a strong seasoning of eccentricity among the inhabitants. Nor have I yet seen any counterargument that acknowledges the pressing problem of high mobility among our neediest students. Mobility is an obvious intellectual embarrassment to the anticurriculum orthodoxy. There are many others, as I have enumerated. The problem for reformers is not intellectual but political.

Some years ago, the mayor of Nashville, the Democrat Phil Bredesen (now governor of Tennessee), flew into Charlottesville with a planeload of top leaders in Nashville's educational community. He had been persuaded by the commonsense logic of the Core Knowledge enterprise and had offered financial inducements to the various interest groups to make Core Knowledge the citywide curriculum. The head of the teachers' union, the superintendent of schools, and the assistant superintendent had all agreed. But when they returned to Nashville, the curriculum specialists and the education professors of the Peabody School of Education at Vanderbilt University rose up against this challenge to their ideas and expertise. To me, the most memorable event in this uprising was the statement of the education school dean, quoted by the local newspaper, the *Tennessean,* to the effect that his colleagues would welcome *any* educational innovation except Core Knowledge. This seemed a very puzzling blanket statement to make. But I have come to understand that an academic curriculum is the one heresy the anti-curriculum creed cannot tolerate. Teachers in Nashville were induced to say they would refuse to teach this reactionary, old-fashioned stuff. Social pressures were brought to bear against Core Knowledge sympathizers, and the Bredesen idea died a quick death. A few years later, when we held an annual Core Knowledge conference in Nashville, a big event with some 2,500 teachers attending, not one teacher from Nashville attended.

The power of enforced intellectual conformity within the education world can be understood only by those who have attended the annual meeting of education professors or enrolled in an American school of education. The following e-mail is typical of messages I sometimes receive from oppressed students in our schools of education. I reprint it with permission but with identifying traits removed.

I am a PhD student in Curriculum Theory at ———. I started in the Socio-Cultural Approaches program but I became disillusioned with methods and theories of teaching and learning that seemed to lack empirical evidence and simply did not resonate as being sensible. . . . I have sat through lecture after lecture where I have heard Professors of Education suggest that children should be "doing" "authentic" science/math/ social studies etc. as opposed to acquiring a strong content knowledge of these discipline areas. . . . I wanted to contact you, Dr. Hirsch, because quite frankly I have become quite disillusioned with my experience. I feel that if the ideologies that I now see as purely self-serving are allowed to permeate into the discourse and practice of mainstream education, then American children, particularly the most in need of the efficacious power of a solid education, will suffer greatly. My experience, however, is that as soon as I question such laudable phrases as "community of learners," "reciprocal teaching," "peer review," or "authentic learning," I am dismissed as at best a hopeless conservative and at worst as an "oppressor" or bigot.

This writer was in a position to resist intellectually only because he had grown up in another country and could see through the established rhetoric. Native-born students are not so fortunate.

In an earlier chapter I noted that American colleges of education are like sectarian churches where heresy is crushed rather than like university departments where debate is encouraged. We need university provosts or presidents who will insist that the education schools appoint a few pro-curriculum professors to counterbalance the anti-curriculum monopoly; who will require public and open debate within the school; who will make sure that students victimized by intellectual tyranny can lodge complaints with university authorities; and who will encourage education professors to engage with other university departments—especially departments of psychology, whose members are, as a rule, less than complimentary about the ideological psychology taught in colleges of education.

Shortly after the mayor of Nashville's efforts, parents in a town in northern Illinois started a citizens' initiative for a city-wide core curriculum. Having become persuaded that a coherent early curriculum would help their children, they secured positive public statements from cognitive scientists and researchers and sponsored a candidate for school superintendent who promised to put the Core Knowledge curriculum in the district's schools. But the entire local educational establishment rose up against these citizens, placing hyperbolic anti-tyranny ads in the newspaper. The incumbent superintendent was even discovered stealing his Core Knowledge rival's vote-for-me signs and carting them away in his car. He was never fined for this civil violation and in fact handily won reelection with his promise not to institute Core Knowledge.

Then there is Hawaii, which is one single statewide education district. Its most successful public school is a Core Knowledge school. Some businesspeople, led by a brave and persistent proponent, David Rolf, led a campaign to make Core Knowledge the basis for the statewide curriculum. Legislators were poised to put this into effect, having been persuaded by the logic of the idea and by the fact that Hawaii is one of the lowest-performing states in education, but the newspaper firestorm that ensued was too intense for any business leader or legislator to withstand. Hawaiian schools remain as they were.

Recently an attempt was made in Texas to introduce explicit subject-matter content into the language-arts standards of the state. Core Knowledge was not in the picture. In fact, no mandated texts were proposed, just a list of certain works *illustrating* the kinds of texts that should be taught. But this list was seen as the camel's nose in the tent. Because the state school board was split between Republicans and Democrats, the question of content was portrayed as a partisan issue, with Republicans for lists, Democrats against them. Right-thinking persons were urged to keep the content-unspecific, process orientation of the present state standards, as in this e-mailed petition to the state board by a teachers' group:

> The amendment, written by a narrow interest group and questionable in its validity . . . is a sterling example of "rote memorization and parroting back facts." It is not education reform—it is education regression. First, it fails to take into account the needs of a diverse student population with a suggested reading list that is unnecessarily limited in its range. Children who are not yet accomplished and sophisticated readers want and need to see themselves in stories. The amendment's methods and materials fail to teach "learning how to learn," a skill that becomes increasingly necessary as technology moves us ever faster into the future. Research has shown time and again that process is what successful teachers teach, and what unsuccessful teachers don't teach. [*This is exactly the opposite of what research shows. EDH*] Process is at the core of the commissioned TEKS [Texas Essential Knowledge and Skills]. Under the amendment, the classroom is teacher-centered, with the teacher feeding information and pupils passively re-

ceiving it. The commissioned TEKS assumes a student-centered classroom, where the teacher creates or designs a learning situation and the students actively engage in their learning: consuming information, thinking, questioning, analyzing, innovating, creating. The teacher then serves as role model, support or coach. . . . The amendment is so flawed, so backward, that it does not warrant consideration. . . . Write to ——— and ask board members to reject the ideas from the amendment and to decide in favor of education reform that will serve all the children of Texas.

These strong statements, it should be noticed, are not opposed to anything as definite as Core Knowledge. They are vigorous objections to the mere listing of illustrative examples such as the following:

Grade 2. Present brief, comprehensive narrative summaries of notable literary selections which are rich in vocabulary e.g., "Harriet Tubman," "Hurt No Living Thing," "Seashell," "Smart," "Caterpillars," "A Christmas Carol," "The Emperor's New Clothes," "How the Camel Got His Hump," "Beauty and the Beast," "The Blind Men and the Elephant," "The Spider and the Fly," "Who Has Seen the Wind?" *Charlotte's Web*, "El Pájaro Cu," *The Courage of Sarah Noble, The Fourth of July Story, The Little House in the Big Woods*.[22]

When I was first writing this section, with the Texas situation still undecided, I found it difficult to believe that the state board would vote for "rote memorization and parroting back facts," for not taking "into account the needs of a diverse student population," and for producing "a generation of people who have difficulty knowing how to think, question or create." (Who knew that "The Blind Men and the Elephant" was so dangerous?) And in fact, the constructive effort by the state board was roundly defeated at a public meeting in the spring of 2008. Teachers and administrators turned out in force to denounce the idea of inserting specific guidance into the state standards—exerting a social and political pressure that the board could not resist.

Renewing Public Education

All over the United States, one may see imposing public school buildings that bespeak the community's commitment to the civic aspirations of the common school. Buildings like Venable Elementary School, in Charlottesville, illustrated here. Why design all these expensive steps and high columns if not to express an almost religious devotion to equality and community through education?

I once attended a meeting in the Regents' room of the New York State Department of Education in Albany. In that sanctuary sit the rulers of the New York public education system, the Regents. Oil portraits of past Regents hang on the walls surrounding the massive table. It is a room worthy of the most opulent corporation or Oxford college. The building's exterior is even more imposing—equal in its own way to the Gothic glory of Oxford's spires. Designed by Henry Hornbostel and erected in 1908, with thirty-six tall columns, it is the most imposing building in Albany, not excluding the state legislature.

Venable Elementary School, 1925, Charlottesville, Virginia.
Photo by E. D. Hirsch, Jr.

The message of such architecture is clear: by educating our citizenry we would create a great nation. It would be a meritocracy—as Jefferson put it, an aristocracy of virtue and talent, not of birth.

That spirit of aspiration and equality animated the creation in 1847 of the Free Academy (later called City College) in New York City. The college's founder, Townsend Harris, proclaimed: "Let the children of the rich and the poor take their seats together and know of no distinction save that of industry, good conduct and intellect"—a phrasing reminiscent of Jefferson, who wished to "avail the commonwealth of those talents and virtues which nature has sown as liberally among the poor as rich."[23] The taxpayers of New York approved the Free Academy project in a statewide referendum. By 1908, the academy had moved uptown and its Great Hall had been erected, on the lines of a cathedral.

State Education Building, 1908, Albany, New York. Courtesy
New York State Department of Education

Front view, Shepard Hall, City College of New York. Courtesy
City College of New York. Photo by Bill Summers

Inside the hall, the stained glass windows high along the nave showed, instead of saints, the seals of various Ivy League colleges. Behind the altar, where I was once privileged to give a talk, is a twenty-two-by-forty-three-foot mural by Edwin Blashfield called *The Graduate*. It depicts a young man being transformed into a shining citizen by what seems to be the goddess of education, after he has ascended from the families and perhaps recent immigrants on the left who are leaning toward him. Also pictured here is an actual graduation at City College in the nave of the cathedral-like building under the vast mural.

For many decades these hopes for democratic education were actually realized. I once asked the historian Diane Ravitch

Edwin Blashfield, *The Graduate* (1908). Courtesy City College of New York. Photo by Bill Summers

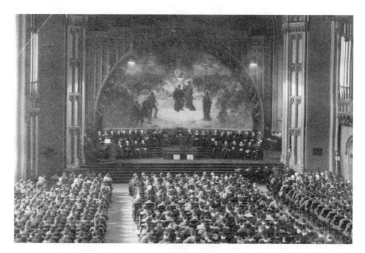

Graduation under *The Graduate.* Courtesy City College of
New York. Photo by Bill Summers

if in fact the New York schools in the 1920s and 1930s, unlike
the New York schools of today, delivered a good education to
all students. She replied: "The schools functioned very well in
the 1920s. There were plenty of kids who left to go to work, but
no one pushed them out. Every community had good or good-
enough schools. There was a curriculum, which everyone
understood. College entry requirements were clear and moti-
vating to those who wanted to go and could afford to go. Discipline was strong."[24]

To get a feel for what happened to our public schools in
later decades, I suggest that the reader put down this book and
go to YouTube to watch a ten-minute movie issued by the
March of Time in the 1940s (search for the keywords *progressive education 1940s*).[25] The announcer triumphantly states
that in tens of thousands of schools across America, children

are no longer memorizing the multiplication table or pursuing dull, bookish studies. They are learning by doing. The movie shows children doing everything except learning the facts of history and math. They are buying and selling items in mock stores, pushing toy trains, and taking field trips to the airport to watch planes fly. The professorial gurus of the movement are shown confidently asserting that this new kind of education is best for confronting the brave future and escaping the dull past. It is amusing to watch William Heard Kilpatrick, sounding like the Southern Baptist preacher that his father was, making these pronouncements with fervor and certitude while his dutiful Teachers College students take copious notes—just the kind of teaching situation he is deploring. The enthusiastic announcer closes by saying that knowledge gained by active doing is learned better and retained longer than bookish rote learning.

By the 1950s, and with blossoming fullness in the 1960s, as the Coleman Report has shown, it was the home and not the school that determined how well educated an American child would become. Apologists tend to view our recent educational decline as having been caused by an influx of Hispanic and black students, thus committing the logical fallacy known as *post hoc ergo propter hoc:*[26] The decline happened after the influx, therefore the influx must have caused it. My alternative explanation is that the influx of Hispanic and black students in the post-desegregation era coincided tragically with the decline of the academic curriculum in the public schools. The history of the contents of our textbooks supports this thesis.[27] Once the academic curriculum had disappeared, no student, rich or poor, who grew up outside an enriched home environment could (except for the odd voracious reader) expect to become well educated. When a school ceases to offer a coherent academic curriculum, only a home-enriched child can thrive academically. Overcoming the anti-curriculum tradition will be a huge task. But in that Texas drama I described a few pages back, which so far has been repeated everywhere the issue has arisen on a large scale, may be seen a possibility for change. Let's suppose the recent public events in Texas had been attended not only by educators but also by citizens who were well informed about scientific misrepresentation and misleading rhetoric in the educational world and who came prepared to take on the anti-curricular forces. There are more citizens than educational lobbyists, and it is citizens who pay the bills. This suggests that the best strategy for solving the problems of American education is not just to erect competing structural arrangements like charter schools but also for greater numbers of citizens and policy makers to challenge received ideas. The chief need for improving American schools, private and public, regular and charter, is an intellectual revolution in public opinion.

How can such a drastic intellectual challenge be mounted on a large scale? One of the two teachers' unions, the American Federation of Teachers, has made a beginning. Its excellent quarterly magazine, *American Educator*, with a circulation of 850,000, has featured in recent years a number of articles on cognitive science and education pointing out that a coherent, cumulative curriculum—knowledge, not how-to drill—is the road to improved student achievement. Most recently, at the very moment when Texas teachers were denouncing specific state standards as being socially unjust and teacher unfriendly, *American Educator* came out with an issue entitled *There's a Gaping Hole in State Standards: What's Missing? Clear, Specific Content.* This is not the first time the late Al Shanker's union has carried on his tradition of looking out for the good of the country against the apparent (but only apparent) interests of teachers. The real interest of teachers, he believed, lies in making the system effective and respected, and his successors at *American Educator* have carried on that tradition. But not even the brave magazine of this influential teachers' union has had much impact on the reigning system of anti-curricular ideas, which is far too entrenched to reform itself. The ability of the educational establishment to resist pro-content ideas had been a remarkable case study in intellectual monopoly within a free society. Strong external pressure on schools and on colleges of education by a better-informed set of politicians and citizens is required.

The need for a common core curriculum in the early grades is far greater in the United States than in other nations that actually have one. Americans move from one place to another in greater numbers than do residents of any other country. As a transethnic nation, we have a greater need for an *invented* common public sphere that is determined not by blood and soil or hearth and home but by transethnic traditions concerning our history, laws, and freedoms. The medium of this public sphere is language, which cannot be disentangled from specific, commonly shared knowledge. That unifying knowledge cannot be learned in our hugely diverse homes, as it is in more homogeneous countries. It can only be learned in our community-centered schools.

One of the gravest disappointments I have felt in the

twenty-five years that I have been actively engaged in educational reform is the frustration of being warmly welcomed by conservatives but shunned by fellow liberals. The connection of the anti-curriculum movement with the Democratic Party is an accident of history, not a logical necessity. All the logic runs the other way. A dominant liberal aim is social justice, and a definite core curriculum in early grades is *necessary* to achieve it. Why should conservatives alone favor solid content while my fellow liberals buy into the rhetoric of the anti-curriculum theology that works against the liberal aims of community and equality? Practical improvement of our public education will require intellectual clarity and a depolarization of this issue. Left and right must get together on the principle of common content. A beginning is being made with a new organization called Common Core that includes Democrats, Republicans, and representatives of the American Federation of Teachers. The unthinkable is starting to be thought and even advocated.

Only a grasp of the accidents of history can enable such change to prevail. The apparently benign idea of natural, child-centered education that took hold at the beginning of the twentieth century came by gradual degrees to vitiate our public education, weaken our county's competence and competitiveness, diminish our solidarity, and destroy equality of opportunity. It has almost nullified two of the most precious founding ideas of the United States, the idea of unity despite our differences and the idea of equality. Nothing of consequence can be done to save public education until the disastrous anti-curriculum theory, which has dominated American schooling for nearly a century, is vigorously set aside. This can be done successfully only if the American public's strong desire for equality, competence, and community can counterbalance the anti-curriculum traditions that have destroyed the community-centered school and badly weakened the public sphere. The tradition of the common school needs to be revived, along with the goals of Jefferson, Rush, Webster, Lincoln, Horace Mann, and, in our own day, John Rawls. The making of Americans that these thinkers viewed as *the* dominant purpose of the public school must be made dominant once again, enriched by the humane traditions of pedagogical practice that the child-centered movement introduced.

On the frieze of the Teachers College Building (1901), facing Broadway at 120th Street in Manhattan, are the names of some of the old heroes of the child-centered movement: Comenius, the seventeenth-century Czech teacher who held that schooling should be made as pleasant as possible for the child, and the nineteenth-century Romantic Swiss and German educators Pestalozzi and Froebel, the inventors of the activity movement who were the direct progenitors of the child-centered movement in the United States. Among the founders of the common school already stands there the name of Horace Mann.[28] Let us keep these names but add to them (at least in our imagination facing Broadway, not the side street) the names of Thomas Jefferson, Benjamin Rush, Noah Webster, and Abraham Lincoln, so that the making of Americans may be again a forthright goal of our public education.

APPENDIX 1

Core Knowledge
History/Geography Thread

Kindergarten
History and Geography: Kindergarten

T E A C H E R S : In kindergarten, children often study aspects of the world around them: the family, the school, the community, etc. The following guidelines are meant to broaden and complement that focus. The goal of studying selected topics in World History in Kindergarten is to foster curiosity and the beginnings of understanding about the larger world outside the child's locality, and about varied civilizations and ways of life. This can be done through a variety of means: story, drama, art, music, discussion, and more.

The study of geography embraces many topics throughout the Core Knowledge Sequence, including topics in history and science. Geographic knowledge includes a spatial sense of the world, an awareness of the physical processes that shape life, a sense of the interactions between humans and their environment, an understanding of the relations between place and culture, and an awareness of the characteristics of specific regions and cultures.

World History and Geography
I. Geography: Spatial Sense
(working with maps, globes, and other geographic tools)

T E A C H E R S : Foster children's geographical awareness through regular work with maps and globes. Have students regularly locate themselves on maps and globes in relation to places they are studying. Children should make and use a simple map of a locality (such as classroom, home, school grounds, "treasure hunt").

189

- Maps and globes: what they represent, how we use them
- Rivers, lakes, and mountains: what they are and how they are represented on maps and globes
- Locate the Atlantic and Pacific Oceans.
- Locate the North and South Poles.

II. An Overview of the Seven Continents

TEACHERS: Help children gain a beginning geographic vocabulary and a basic sense of how we organize and talk about the world by giving names to some of the biggest pieces of land. Introduce children to the seven continents through a variety of media (tracing, coloring, relief maps, etc.), and associate the continents with familiar wildlife, landmarks, etc. (for example, penguins in Antarctica; the Eiffel Tower in Europe). Throughout the school year, reinforce names and locations of continents when potential connections arise in other disciplines (for example, connect Grimm's fairy tales to Europe; voyage of Pilgrims to Europe and North America; story of "Momotaro—Peach Boy" to Asia [Japan]; study of Native Americans to North America).

- Identify and locate the seven continents on a map and globe:

  Asia

  Europe

  Africa

  North America

  South America

  Antarctica

  Australia

American History and Geography

TEACHERS: The study of American history begins in grades K-2 with a brief overview of major events and figures, from the earliest days to recent times. A more in-depth, chronological study of American history begins again in grade 3 and continues onward. The term "American" here generally, but not always, refers to the lands that became the United States. Other topics regarding North, Central, and South America may be found in the World History and Geography sections of this Sequence.

I. Geography

- Name and locate the town, city, or community, as well as the state where you live.

- Locate North America, the continental United States, Alaska, and Hawaii.

II. Native American Peoples, Past and Present

TEACHERS: As children progress through the grades of the Core Knowledge Sequence, they will learn about many different Native American peoples in many different regions. In kindergarten, study at least one specific group of Native Americans: explore how they lived, what they wore and ate, the homes they lived in, their beliefs and stories, etc., and also explore the current status of the tribe or nation. You might explore a local or regional tribe or nation, and compare it with one far away.

- Become familiar with the people and ways of life of at least one Native American tribe or nation, such as:

  Pacific Northwest: Kwakiutl, Chinook

  Plateau: Nez Perce

  Great Basin: Shoshone, Ute

  Southwest: Dine [Navajo], Hopi, Apache

  Plains: Blackfoot, Comanche, Crow, Kiowa, Dakota, Cheyenne, Arapaho, Lakota (Sioux)

  Northeast: Huron, Iroquois

Eastern Woodlands: Cherokee, Seminole, Delaware, Susquehanna, Mohican, Massachusett, Wampanoag, Powhatan

III. Early Exploration and Settlement

A. The voyage of Columbus in 1492

- Queen Isabella and King Ferdinand of Spain
- The Niña, Pinta, and Santa Maria
- Columbus's mistaken identification of "Indies" and "Indians"
- The idea of what was, for Europeans, a "New World"

B. The Pilgrims

- The Mayflower
- Plymouth Rock
- Thanksgiving Day celebration

C. July 4, "Independence Day"

- The "birthday" of our nation
- Democracy (rule of the people): Americans wanted to rule themselves instead of being ruled by a faraway king.
- Some people were not free: slavery in early America

IV. Presidents, Past and Present

TEACHERS: Introduce children to famous presidents, and discuss with them such questions as: What is the president? How does a person become president? Who are some of our most famous presidents, and why?

- George Washington

  The "Father of His Country"

  Legend of George Washington and the cherry tree

- Thomas Jefferson, author of Declaration of Independence

- Abraham Lincoln

  Humble origins

  "Honest Abe"

- Theodore Roosevelt

- Current United States president

V. Symbols and Figures

- Recognize and become familiar with the significance of

  American flag

  Statue of Liberty

  Mount Rushmore

  The White House

First Grade

History and Geography: Grade 1

TEACHERS: In first grade, children often study aspects of the world around them: the family, the school, the community, etc. The following guidelines are meant to broaden and complement that focus. The goal of studying selected topics in World History in first grade is to foster curiosity and the beginnings of understanding about the larger world outside the child's locality, and about varied civilizations and ways of life. This can be done through a variety of means: story, drama, art, music, discussion, and more.

The study of geography embraces many topics throughout the Core Knowledge Sequence, including topics in history and science. Geographic knowledge embraces a spatial sense of the world, an awareness of the physical processes that shape life, a sense of the interactions between humans and their environment, an understanding of the relations between place and culture, and an awareness of the characteristics of specific regions and cultures.

World History and Geography

I. Geography

A. Spatial Sense (Working with Maps, Globes, and Other Geographic Tools)

TEACHERS: Foster children's geographical awareness through regular work with maps and globes. Have students regularly locate themselves on maps and globes in relation to places they are studying.

- Name your continent, country, state, and community.

- Understand that maps have keys or legends with symbols and their uses.

- Find directions on a map: east, west, north, south.

- Identify major oceans: Pacific, Atlantic, Indian, Arctic.

- Review the seven continents: Asia, Europe, Africa, North America, South America, Antarctica, Australia.

- Locate: Canada, United States, Mexico, Central America.

- Locate: the Equator, Northern Hemisphere, Southern Hemisphere, North and South Poles.

B. Geographical terms and features

- peninsula, harbor, bay, island

II. Early Civilizations

TEACHERS: As you introduce children to early civilizations, keep in mind the question, What is civilization? Help children see recurring features such as settling down, agriculture, building towns and cities, and learning how to write.

A. Mesopotamia: The "Cradle of Civilization"

- Importance of Tigris and Euphrates Rivers
- Development of writing, why writing is important to the development of civilization
- Code of Hammurabi (early code of laws), why rules and laws are important to the development of civilization

B. Ancient Egypt

- Geography

  Africa

  Sahara Desert
- Importance of Nile River, floods and farming
- Pharaohs

  Tutankhamen

  Hatshepsut, woman pharaoh
- Pyramids and mummies, animal gods, Sphinx
- Writing: hieroglyphics

C. History of World Religions

TEACHERS: Since religion is a shaping force in the story of civilization, the Core Knowledge Sequence introduces children in the early grades to major world religions, beginning with a focus on geography and major symbols and figures. The purpose is not to explore matters of theology but to provide a basic vocabulary for understanding many events and ideas in history. The goal is to familiarize, not proselytize; to be descriptive, not prescriptive. The tone should be one of respect and balance: no religion should be disparaged by implying that it is a thing of the past. To the question, "Which one is true?" an appropriate response is: "People of different faiths believe different things to be true. The best people to guide you on this right now are your parents or someone at home."

- Judaism

  Belief in one God

  Story of the Exodus: Moses leads the Hebrews out of Egypt

  Israel, Chanukah, Star of David, Torah, synagogue

- Christianity

  Christianity grew out of Judaism

  Jesus, meaning of "messiah"

  Christmas and Easter, symbol of the cross

- Islam

  Originated in Arabia, since spread worldwide

  Followers are called Muslims

  Allah, Muhammad, Makkah, Qur'an, mosque

  Symbol of crescent and star (found on the flags of many mainly Islamic nations)

III. Modern Civilization and Culture: Mexico

A. Geography

- North American continent, locate Mexico relative to Canada and the United States

- Central America, Yucatan Peninsula
- Pacific Ocean, Gulf of Mexico, Rio Grande
- Mexico City

B. Culture

- Indian and Spanish heritage
- Traditions: fiesta, piñata
- National holiday: September 16, Independence Day

American History and Geography

TEACHERS: The study of American history begins in grades K-2 with a brief overview of major events and figures, from the earliest days to recent times. A more in-depth, chronological study of American history begins again in grade 3 and continues onward. The term "American" here generally, but not always, refers to the lands that became the United States. Other topics regarding North, Central, and South America may be found in the World History and Geography sections of this Sequence.

I. Early People and Civilizations

A. The Earliest People: Hunters and Nomads

- Crossing the land bridge from Asia to North America

  From hunting to farming

  Gradual development of early towns and cities

B. Maya, Inca, and Aztec Civilizations

TEACHERS: Children will study the Maya, Inca, and Aztec civilizations in detail in grade 5. First grade teachers should examine the fifth grade guidelines to see how these topics build in the later grade.

Here, introduce children to these civilizations. Though it is historically accurate to note the warlike nature of the Maya and Aztecs, it is recommended that mention of the practice of human sacrifice be left to the fifth grade.

- Maya in Mexico and Central America
- Aztecs in Mexico

  Moctezuma (also called Montezuma)

  Tenochtitlan (Mexico City)
- Inca in South America (Peru, Chile)

  Cities in the Andes, Machu Picchu

II. Early Exploration and Settlement

A. Columbus

TEACHERS: Review from kindergarten the story of Columbus's voyage in 1492.

B. The Conquistadors

- The search for gold and silver
- Hernán Cortés and the Aztecs
- Francisco Pizarro and the Inca
- Diseases devastate Native American population

C. English Settlers

- The story of the Lost Colony

  Sir Walter Raleigh

  Virginia Dare

- Virginia

  Jamestown

  Captain John Smith

  Pocahontas and Powhatan

- Slavery, plantations in Southern colonies

- Massachusetts

  Pilgrims, Mayflower, Thanksgiving Day

  Massachusetts Bay Colony, the Puritans

III. From Colonies to Independence: The American Revolution

TEACHERS: The American Revolution will be studied in greater depth and detail in grade 4. First grade teachers should examine the fourth grade guidelines to see how these topics build in the later grade. It is recommended that first grade teachers focus on the topics specified here, and leave for fourth grade the more detailed study of the Revolution. In first grade, emphasize the story of how we went from colonies to an independent nation.

- Locate the original thirteen colonies.

- The Boston Tea Party

- Paul Revere's ride, "One if by land, two if by sea"

- Minutemen and Redcoats, the "shot heard round the world"

- Thomas Jefferson and the Declaration of Independence, "We hold these truths to be self-evident, that all men are created equal. . . ."

- Fourth of July

- Benjamin Franklin: patriot, inventor, writer

- George Washington: from military commander to our first president

  Martha Washington

  Our national capital city named Washington
- Legend of Betsy Ross and the flag

IV. Early Exploration of the American West

TEACHERS: America's westward growth will be studied in grade 2 and in greater depth and detail in grade 5. First grade teachers should examine the second and fifth grade guidelines to see how these topics build in later grades.

- Daniel Boone and the Wilderness Road
- The Louisiana Purchase

  Explorations of Lewis and Clark

  Sacagawea
- Geography: Locate the Appalachian Mountains, the Rocky Mountains, and the Mississippi River.

V. Symbols and Figures

- Recognize and become familiar with the significance of

  Liberty Bell

  Current United States president

  American flag

  Eagle

Second Grade
History and Geography: Grade 2

TEACHERS: In second grade, children often study aspects of the world around them: the family, the school, the community, etc. The following guidelines are meant to broaden and complement that focus. The goal of studying selected topics in World History in second grade is to foster curiosity and the beginnings of understanding about the larger world outside the child's locality, and about varied civilizations and ways of life. This can be done through a variety of means: story, drama, art, music, discussion, and more.

The study of geography embraces many topics throughout the Core Knowledge Sequence, including topics in history and science. Geographic knowledge includes a spatial sense of the world, an awareness of the physical processes that shape life, a sense of the interactions between humans and their environment, an understanding of the relations between place and culture, and an awareness of the characteristics of specific regions and cultures.

World History and Geography

I. Geography

A. Spatial Sense (Working with Maps, Globes, and Other Geographic Tools)

TEACHERS:

- Name your continent, country, state, and community.
- Understand that maps have keys or legends with symbols and their uses.
- Find directions on a map: east, west, north, south.
- Identify major oceans: Pacific, Atlantic, Indian, Arctic.
- The seven continents: Asia, Europe, Africa, North America, South America, Antarctica, Australia.
- Locate: Canada, United States, Mexico, Central America.
- Locate: the Equator, Northern Hemisphere and Southern Hemisphere, North and South Poles.

B. Geographical terms and features

TEACHERS:

- coast, valley, prairie, desert, oasis

II. Early Civilizations: Asia

T E A C H E R S : Since religion is a shaping force in the story of civilization, the Core Knowledge Sequence introduces children in the early grades to major world religions, beginning with a focus on geography and major symbols and figures. The purpose is not to explore matters of theology but to provide a basic vocabulary for understanding many events and ideas in history. The goal is to familiarize, not proselytize; to be descriptive, not prescriptive. The tone should be one of respect and balance: no religion should be disparaged by implying that it is a thing of the past. To the question, "Which one is true?" an appropriate response is: "People of different faiths believe different things to be true. The best people to guide you on this right now are your parents or someone at home."

A. Geography of Asia

- The largest continent, with the most populous countries in the world

- Locate: China, India, Japan

B. India

- Indus River and Ganges River

- Hinduism

  Brahma, Vishnu, Shiva

  Many holy books, including the Rig Veda

- Buddhism

  Prince Siddhartha becomes Buddha, "the Enlightened One"

  Buddhism begins as an outgrowth of Hinduism in India, and then spreads through many countries in Asia.

  King Asoka (also spelled Ashoka)

C. China

TEACHERS: Students will study China again in grade 4. Second grade teachers should examine the fourth grade guidelines to see how these topics build in the later grade.

- Yellow (Huang He) and Yangtze (Chang Jiang) Rivers
- Teachings of Confucius (for example, honor your ancestors)
- Great Wall of China
- Invention of paper
- Importance of silk
- Chinese New Year

III. Modern Civilization and Culture: Japan

A. Geography

- Locate relative to continental Asia: "land of the rising sun"
- A country made up of islands; four major islands
- Pacific Ocean, Sea of Japan
- Mt. Fuji
- Tokyo

B. Culture

- Japanese flag
- Big modern cities, centers of industry and business
- Traditional craft: origami
- Traditional costume: kimono

IV. Ancient Greece

T E A C H E R S : Students will study Greece again in grade 6, with a focus on the legacy of ideas from ancient Greece and Rome.

- Geography: Mediterranean Sea and Aegean Sea, Crete

- Sparta

- Persian Wars: Marathon and Thermopylae

- Athens as a city-state: the beginnings of democracy

- Olympic games

- Worship of gods and goddesses

- Great thinkers: Socrates, Plato, and Aristotle

- Alexander the Great

American History and Geography

T E A C H E R S : The study of American history begins in grades K-2 with a brief overview of major events and figures, from the earliest days to recent times. A more in-depth, chronological study of American history begins again in grade 3 and continues onward. The term "American" here generally, but not always, refers to the lands that became the United States. Other topics regarding North, Central, and South America may be found in the World History and Geography sections of this Sequence.

I. American Government: The Constitution

T E A C H E R S : Through analogies to familiar settings—the family, the school, the community—discuss some basic questions regarding American government, such as: What is government? What are some basic functions of American government? (Making and enforcing laws; settling disputes; protecting rights and liberties, etc.) Only basic questions need to be addressed at this grade level. In fourth grade students will examine in more detail specific issues and institutions of American government, including, for example, the separation of powers, and the relation between state and federal government.

- American government is based on the Constitution, the highest law of our land.

- James Madison, the "Father of the Constitution"

- Government by the consent of the governed: "We the people"

II. The War of 1812

- President James Madison and Dolley Madison

- British impressment of American sailors

- Old Ironsides

- British burn the White House

- Fort McHenry, Francis Scott Key, and "The Star-Spangled Banner"

- Battle of New Orleans, Andrew Jackson

III. Westward Expansion

TEACHERS: Students will study Westward Expansion in greater depth and detail in grade 5. Second grade teachers should examine the fifth grade guidelines to see how these topics build in the later grade. It is recommended that second grade teachers keep their focus on the people and events specified here, and leave for fifth grade the figures and ideas specified for that grade.

A. Pioneers Head West

- New means of travel

  Robert Fulton, invention of the steamboat

  Erie Canal

Railroads: the Transcontinental Railroad

- Routes west: wagon trains on the Oregon Trail
- The Pony Express

B. Native Americans

- Sequoyah and the Cherokee alphabet
- Forced removal to reservations: the "Trail of Tears"
- Some Native Americans displaced from their homes and ways of life by railroads (the "iron horse")
- Effect of near extermination of buffalo on Plains Indians

IV. The Civil War

TEACHERS: Students will study the Civil War in greater depth and detail in grade 5. Second grade teachers should examine the fifth grade guidelines to see how these topics build in the later grade.

- Controversy over slavery
- Harriet Tubman, the "underground railroad"
- Northern v. Southern states: Yankees and Rebels
- Ulysses S. Grant and Robert E. Lee
- Clara Barton, "Angel of the Battlefield," founder of American Red Cross
- President Abraham Lincoln: keeping the Union together
- Emancipation Proclamation and the end of slavery

V. Immigration and Citizenship

TEACHERS: Students will study Immigration and Urbanization in greater depth and detail in grade 6.

Second grade teachers should examine the sixth grade American History guidelines to see how these topics build in the later grade. In second grade, it is recommended that teachers use narrative, biography, and other accessible means to introduce children to the idea that many people have come to America (and continue to come here) from all around the world, for many reasons: to find freedom, to seek a better life, to leave behind bad conditions in their native lands, etc. Discuss with children: What is an immigrant? Why do people leave their home countries to make a new home in America? What is it like to be a newcomer in America? What hardships have immigrants faced? What opportunities have they found?

- America perceived as a "land of opportunity"

- The meaning of "e pluribus unum" (a national motto you can see on the back of coins)

- Ellis Island and the significance of the Statue of Liberty

- Millions of newcomers to America

  Large populations of immigrants settle in major cities (such as New York, Chicago, Philadelphia, Detroit, Cleveland, Boston, San Francisco)

- The idea of citizenship

  What it means to be a citizen of a nation

  American citizens have certain rights and responsibilities (for example, voting, eligible to hold public office, paying taxes)

  Becoming an American citizen (by birth, naturalization)

VI. Civil Rights

TEACHERS:

- Susan B. Anthony and the right to vote
- Eleanor Roosevelt and civil rights and human rights

- Mary McLeod Bethune and educational opportunity
- Jackie Robinson and the integration of major league base-ball
- Rosa Parks and the bus boycott in Montgomery, Alabama
- Martin Luther King, Jr. and the dream of equal rights for all
- Cesar Chavez and the rights of migrant workers

VII. Geography of the Americas

A. North America

- North America: Canada, United States, Mexico
- The United States

  Fifty states: 48 contiguous states, plus Alaska and Hawaii

  Territories

  Mississippi River

  Appalachian and Rocky Mountains

  Great Lakes
- Atlantic and Pacific Oceans, Gulf of Mexico, Caribbean Sea, West Indies
- Central America

B. South America

- Brazil: largest country in South America, Amazon River, rain forests
- Peru and Chile: Andes Mountains
- Locate: Venezuela, Colombia, Ecuador

- Bolivia: named after Simon Bolivar, "The Liberator"
- Argentina: the Pampas
- Main languages: Spanish and (in Brazil) Portuguese

VIII. Symbols and Figures

- Recognize and become familiar with the significance of

  U.S. flag: current and earlier versions

  Statue of Liberty

  Lincoln Memorial

APPENDIX 2

Content Is Skill, Skill Content

By the time *A Nation at Risk* was published in 1983, cognitive psychology had achieved a degree of consensus about the fundamental nature of academic skills. Yet the science of psychology was not often alluded to in *A Nation at Risk*. Even today, twenty-five years later, there is little crossover between cognitive science and educational policy. *A Nation at Risk* simply assumed that gaining an academic skill such as reading or reckoning is independent of the specific curricular content through which the skill is taught. This formalistic conception continues to dominate American educational circles. It is a misleading oversimplification that will have to be corrected if our schools are successfully to teach "higher-order" skills.

The main purpose of this appendix is to summarize key features of the present scientific consensus on the nature of academic skills and to indicate what that consensus implies for achieving the "higher-order skills" that *A Nation at Risk* called for in the early grades. My strategy will be to comment briefly on a few key propositions that, taken together, summarize the current scientific understanding of academic skills. For brevity, my examples will come from reading, but the underlying principles apply also to math, and indeed to any academic skill.

I will first state the five propositions. Then I shall briefly explain each of them. (For bibliographical references and general illumination, see Daniel T. Willingham, *Why Don't Students Like School?: A Cognitive Scientist Answers Questions about How the Mind Works and What It Means for the Classroom* [New York: Jossey-Bass/Wiley, 2009]; and Willingham, *Cognition: The Thinking Animal,* 2nd ed. [Upper Saddle River, NJ : Pearson Prentice Hall, 2004].)

1.   The character of an academic skill is constrained by the narrow limitations of working memory.

2. Academic skills have two components: procedures and contents.

3. Procedural skills such as turning letters into sounds must initially be learned as content along with other content necessary to higher-order skills.

4. An advance in skill, whether in procedure or content, entails an advance in speed of processing.

5. A higher-order academic skill such as reading comprehension requires prior knowledge of domain-specific content; the higher-order skill for that domain does not readily transfer to other content domains.

These well-established principles taken together constitute a refutation of the formalistic conception of academic skills. They explain why national systems of early education that stress a coherent approach to content succeed in teaching higher-order skills such as math problem-solving more effectively than does our system, which, although it explicitly stresses higher-order skills, does so on the incorrect assumption that they are formal procedures that can be learned through arbitrary contents and transferred to new content domains. This is a mistake of historic proportions that partly explains the relatively poor performance of our schools in international comparisons.

The Five Principles

1. The character of an academic skill is constrained by the narrow limitations of working memory.

The conscious activity of the mind occurs within a narrow window of time, lasting a very few seconds, in which we can manipulate a very small number of mental objects before they disappear into forgetfulness. These limitations of consciousness cannot be overcome directly. Acquiring a skill means acquiring ways of indirectly circumventing the limitations of working memory for the purposes at hand. This is the most fundamental and important principle for understanding the nature of academic skills.

Consider the difference in mental capacity between a practiced reader and a beginning first grader who is painstakingly, slowly parsing out T-H-E-C-A-T-I-S-O-N-T-H-E-M-A-T. What is the difference in raw mental capacity between that child and practiced readers? We find that the child's functional mental operations are equal to or even exceed our own. For instance, the child's ability to remember a set of unfamiliar sounds or shapes is equal to ours, and the child's reaction time may be even faster than ours. The child's basic operational machinery—the hardware so to speak—is as good as or better than our own.

It follows that our ability to read "The cat is on the mat" is not a consequence of an enhanced raw ability that has made our mental muscles bigger and stronger or has given us a more powerful central processing unit. Our ability is rather the consequence of our acquiring some specific software that allows us to transform an arduous task for the child into a task that is as easy for us as falling off a log, despite the fact that neither our working memory nor our reaction time is better than the child's. Our ability effortlessly to convert visual symbols into words is an acquired system by means of which we are able cleverly to circumvent the still-unyielding constraints of working memory.

On this basic fact hang all the law and the prophets of educational doctrine relative to skills. The conscious mind, where "higher-order" skills mostly take place, is limited by a universal, highly democratic constraint called "working memory" whose narrow limits are on average the same for child and adult, rich and poor. It is the small window of present-tense consciousness and attention. It is the "place" where we put things together and create meaning, where we solve problems and process language. Within its small temporal extent, which lasts just a few seconds, we are able to manipulate only a very small number of sensations, sounds, or symbols.

In the 1950s, the cognitive psychologist George Miller wrote a famous article about the limitations of working memory called "The Magical Number Seven Plus or Minus Two." (Some now believe that the true limit of working memory varies according to the temporal constraints of number of syllables required to name the items.) The acquiring of academic skills—including, notably, acquiring a big vocabulary—consists of building efficient mental systems that enable us, despite this very constrained bottleneck, to perform huge feats of analysis and synthesis.

A famous experiment conducted by the Dutch psychologist Adrian de Groot illustrated this universal bottleneck in human processing skills. He noticed that chess grand masters have a remarkable skill that we amateurs cannot emulate. They can glance for five seconds at a complex midgame chess position of twenty-five pieces, perform an intervening task of some sort, and then reconstruct on a blank chessboard the entire chess position without making any mistakes. Performance on this task correlates almost perfectly with one's chess ranking. Grand masters make no mistakes, masters a very few, and amateurs can get just five or six pieces right. (Remember the magical number seven, plus or minus two!)

On a brilliant hunch, de Groot then performed the same experiment with twenty-five chess pieces in positions that, instead of being taken from an actual chess game, were just placed at random on the board. Under these new conditions, the performances of the three different groups—grand masters, masters, and novices—were all exactly the same, each group remembering just five or six pieces correctly.

The experiment suggests the skill difference between a master reader who can easily reproduce the sixteen letters of "the cat is on the mat" and a beginning reader who has trouble reproducing the same letters: t-h-e-c-a-t-i-s-o-n-t-h-e-m-a-t. If, instead of providing expert and child with that sentence, we change the task and ask them to reproduce a sequence of random letters, the performance of the first grader and the master reader will become much closer. If the sixteen letters had been "rtu kjs vb fw nqi pgf," the expert would exhibit little skill advantage over the novice, and on average neither will get more than a short sequence of the letters right.

Practiced readers, chess grand masters, and other experts do not possess any special, formal mental skills that novices lack, and they do not perform any better than novices on formally similar yet unfamiliar tasks. Nonetheless, experts are able to perform remarkable feats of memory with real-world situations such as midgame chess positions and actual sentences. How do they manage?

The sentence "The cat is on the mat" consists of six words that are easily remembered, and expert readers can easily reproduce the sixteen letters, not because the letters are individually remembered, but because they are reconstructed from prior knowledge of written English. What de Groot found, and what subsequent research has continually confirmed, is that the difference in higher-order skill between a novice and an expert lies not in mental muscles but in what de Groot called "erudition," a vast store of available, relevant, previously acquired knowledge.

Despite the narrow limitations of working memory, the wealth of contents that can be manipulated by experts through this previously acquired "erudition" is immense. If I already know a lot about baseball, the term "sacrifice fly" can represent a page or two of exposition. Such shorthand representation is a chief time-saving technique of higher-order skills. A short, manageable element (such as a phrase) can represent a much larger complex of already-learned meaning. The phrase "World War II" is short and therefore easily remembered, but the content represented by the phrase is enormous. It cannot be grasped by those who, however skillful in other ways, lack that relevant knowledge. By the time someone had learned the content needed to grasp "World War II," the immediate task would have long disappeared from working memory. The phrase can be understood and communicated only by those who already share the relevant knowledge and associations.

I use this example as a rapid way of indicating why an academic skill like reading depends on learning much more than the foundational ability to form sounds from symbols, turn the sounds into words, and combine the words in sentences. Although such formal skills are critically important, they are quite insufficient to comprehend a passage about World War II in the absence of relevant already-learned background knowledge. A shorthand way of saying this is that the skill of reading (and listening) depends on, among other things, a prior knowledge of what most of the words in a text mean and refer to.

This example can be generalized. A skill depends on prior possession of specifically relevant content knowledge that enables the mind to circumvent the strict limits of working memory. Academic skills cannot be isolated from the possession of specifically relevant content knowledge.

The subsequent four principles are clarifications of this essential insight.

2. *Academic skills have two components: procedures and contents.*

Procedural skills correspond roughly to activities that have become automatic and unconscious, content skills to activities that are conscious. A complex skill like reading is composed of both "procedural" elements like decoding and content ("declarative") elements like vocabulary knowledge.

I type these words under a disadvantage. I never learned a system of touch typing. Still, because I have performed this activity so many times, I type fairly fast. Finding the right key takes up little of my working memory. I never have to ask myself where a letter on the keyboard is; I just hit it without thinking. This is the very model of learning a procedural skill. The activity becomes automatic and unconscious because it is often repeated and nearly invariant. The letters on the keyboard do not move around from one typing occasion to the next. Similarly, the procedural skills of reading—rapid eye movements from left to right and from line to line, automatic calculation of the highest letter-sound probabilities ("decoding")—these remain fairly stable and repeatable from one reading event to another and are therefore good candidates for being turned into unconscious, procedural skills.

The so-called basic skills of reading and math are largely of this procedural sort. It is essential that these skills be mastered so that working memory can occupy itself with non-repeated, content-based skills such as reading comprehension. Given the constraints of working memory, any mental space that is consciously concerned with decoding and identifying words will occupy precious mental space that will be denied to higher-order skills. Under procedural skills may also be listed the additional component of "metacognitive knowledge." This is the unconscious self-monitoring with which we conduct a task, such as asking myself: "What is this author trying to tell me?" Or "If that is the title, then it must be a theme to be emphasized."

These "basic" skills, when mastered and rendered unconscious and automatic, are regarded by psychologists as constituting a separate system that deserves the separate name "procedural." It should be emphasized, however, that procedural skills are not inherently independent of content. They do not start out as part of a separate system. Before my typing became fast, automatic, and unconscious, it was conscious, slow, and error-prone. This is the usual pattern for learning procedural skills. Before a child masters the automatic decoding of print into speech sounds, many hours of conscious and laborious content-filled activities have to be gone through. Such skills are contents before they are procedures. In the early grades, the regularities and probabilities behind the procedural skills are themselves an important content of schooling. But the fact that such pre-procedural skills are "basic" doesn't mean they are the only important content of early schooling—a point that deserves mention as a third principle.

3. Procedural skills such as turning letters into sounds must initially be learned as content along with other content necessary to higher-order skills.

Efforts to learn procedural skills such as the decoding of letters into words are at first slow and uncertain because of the narrow limitations of working memory. Some procedural skills like decoding become speedy and automatic only after years of practice. The case is different with content-based skills such as vocabulary knowledge. These so-called declarative elements can be learned rapidly with few exposures and must expand greatly to achieve greater skill. These relevant declarative elements are the chief components of "higher-order" abilities. Knowledge of the broad content that is relevant to the general reading demanded by the modern world should be gained steadily from the earliest years of schooling along with procedural skills.

The complex skill of reading comprehension is a combination of both types of skills. Reading skill consists of a relatively small store of unconscious procedural skills accompanied by a massive, slowly built-up store of conscious declarative skills (such as vocabulary). If school time is to be spent effectively in early grades, the massive buildup of content knowledge that is essential to higher-order skills must not be subordinated to the slow multiyear buildup of foundational procedural skills. For maximum effectiveness, both kinds of skill-learning should go on simultaneously.

The procedural/declarative distinction used by psychologists clarifies the dual, unconscious/conscious character of academic skills. The duality suggests why our schools have been mistaken in assuming that reading skill can be reliably built up simply by wide practice and frequent exposure to arbitrary sorts of content. This conception does work for procedural tasks like eye movements and decoding that are relatively invariant from one occasion to another. But exposure to arbitrary content cannot reliably build up the knowledge and vocabulary that is the foundation of higher-order reading skill, because these "declarative" elements are not the same from one task to another. They require conscious attention in working memory.

It is true that broad content knowledge can be built up over time simply from wide reading. Given world enough and time, the reading of many and varied books over many years can yield a good general education—witness Abraham Lincoln. But the Lincoln method is not generalizable. Achieving competence in higher-order, knowledge-based skills such as reading comprehension is a difficult and time-consuming process that the schools need to foster in a time-effective way. Exposing students to declarative content in a hit-or-miss fashion leaves many behind. Exposing them to content in a coherent sequence, as many national systems do, securely provides all students with the content knowledge they need to be competent readers.

Bringing all students to competence in higher-order skills is a fundamental responsibility of the schools of a democracy. If we follow out the implications of the scientific consensus, our schools are duty-bound to adopt a coherent, rational, and sequenced approach to content and vocabulary knowledge—not the content-indifferent approach allowed by a mistakenly formal, purely procedural conception of "higher-order" skills.

4. *An advance in skill, whether in procedure or content, means an advance in speed of processing.*

For repeated, procedural activities such as translating visual symbols to sounds, speed is increased by "automaticity." For content skills such as reading comprehension, speed is increased by "chunking."

An advance in skill requires an advance in speed because the contents of working memory begin to disintegrate and dissolve after a few seconds. Correlating the things that we are thinking or reading about has to be done fast before the elements disappear. Working memory imposes an unforgiving temporal limitation on what we can attend to before the elements of thought evaporate.

The magnitude of what we are able to accomplish in this small window of conscious attention depends first on our causing the procedural aspects of the task to take up less and less mental time and space. We can attend only to a few things at a time, so if we attend to the basic process, we can't attend to much else. The more automatically and rapidly we can turn letters into words and sentences, the more of them we can attend to. The beginning reader cannot remember the sixteen letters of

THECATISONTHEMAT because his or her working memory gets filled up by the conscious process of attaching names and sounds to the visual symbols, leaving no mental space for active attention to the letter sequence itself. Speed is of the essence. The higher-order processes cannot begin to function well until these underlying processes have become fast and automatic.

Once the underlying processes of reading have become fast and automatic, we must still be able to deal with the substance of what the decoded words signify. Being able effortlessly to turn WORLDWARII into WORLD WAR TWO doesn't count for much if we don't comprehend what the phrase means. In this sphere of declarative content, speed also counts for a great deal. The rapid availability of a phrase's meaning enables us actively to combine that meaning with other meanings before the elements dissolve into oblivion.

The general skill of reading comprehension correlates very highly with the possession of a broad, quickly available general vocabulary, which is unsurprising since vocabulary knowledge is a component of the skill of reading comprehension. A vocabulary item like WORLD WAR TWO can be unpacked by a comprehending reader into a large number of implicitly included meanings like "Axis Powers," "Allies," "1939–1945," "Holocaust," "Atom Bomb," and so on, and these can themselves be further unpacked. All these meanings are implicitly included in the phrase, but the phrase itself is so compact that it can be manipulated with other large complexes of meaning before the elements dissipate.

The concentration of complex meaning into a simple, small packet that can be accommodated in working memory is the chief trick of the mind in higher-order skills. When psychologists first began experimenting with the limits of working memory, they found that a chief device for improving performance was "chunking"—that is, turning a large number of discrete items into a small number of chunks. If you want to remember the telephone number 7265346519, you will do well to turn these eleven discrete items into three chunks: 726-534-6519.

In order for us humans to think effectively, the elements that we attend to must be grasped rapidly and therefore must be few in number. Later on, the numerous implications of those few elements can be unpacked and analyzed at leisure. It was rapid concentration of meaning that de Groot's chess masters engaged in—a kind of chess vocabulary, whether or not formed into words—when they observed a midgame position. They immediately identified a familiar structure that could have been named, say, "Queen's Pawn Gambit Declined, Lasker Variation." Later they could unpack this quasi-vocabulary item and reconstruct the position with perfect fidelity. The fundamental need of the mind for such speedy meaning-concentration explains why higher-order skills require the possession of relevant prior knowledge and its associated vocabulary.

5. *A higher-order academic skill such as reading comprehension requires prior knowledge of domain-specific content; the higher-order skill for that domain does not readily transfer as a skill to other content domains.*

De Groot showed that being an expert in chess does not improve one's memory for randomized chess positions. Following out the implications of that discovery, psychologists have found that being expert in chess is even less likely to improve one's skills in areas that are still more remote from chess, such as math problem-solving or the ability to think logically about politics. A famous example was Bobby Fisher. He was one of the greatest chess grand masters America has produced, with unparalleled critical thinking skills for analyzing chess strategy, but with famously poor critical-thinking skills in the affairs of everyday life. Michael Jordan was another who was not able to transfer his brilliant athletic skills from basketball to baseball, though such common elements as hand-eye coordination would have helped him since such basic procedural skills remained somewhat stable from task to task.

Being good at one mental skill does not necessarily train the mind to be skilled in other domains. This could be called the "principle of non-transferability." It is one of the solidest findings of psychology, confirmed and reconfirmed many times—tested so often possibly because it has been such a surprising and unwelcome finding. People who have just finished a course in logic are barely more logical than those who have never taken such a course. People who have been carefully trained how to solve a problem in one domain are rarely able to solve a problem that has identical structure but lies in a different domain. Those who are skilled at diverse tasks in various domains are people who have managed to acquire broad general knowledge that includes knowledge relevant to those diverse domains. Such generalized skill is in fact a practical aim of a broad, general education. Students who score well on the verbal SAT invariably possess a broad vocabulary that represents broad general knowledge—which is hardly surprising since the verbal SAT is essentially an advanced vocabulary test.

The so-called higher-order skills are therefore those that are least susceptible to transfer. They are the most dependent on domain-specific knowledge. All of the examples and analyses in this chapter hint why higher skills are so dependent upon specific knowledge. They show that problem solving and critical thinking are not mental muscles. They are not abstract rules of operation. If remembering chess positions had been based on internalized rules, then the grand masters would have been able to apply them (as they were not) to a completely random chess position. There do exist internalized rules of operation in a skill, of course, but these never concern aspects that we call "higher-order" skills. They are more like the rules of grammar in a language. These stable grammar rules transfer from one sentence and domain to another, because they are relatively invariant. But they are also relatively basic. A six-year-old has already internalized most of the intricacies of grammar rules. What the six-year-old lacks is world knowledge and its associated vocabulary. Such knowledge is not imparted by schools that place their educational faith in the power of formal skills, and the assumption that they will empower a child to acquire knowledge and vocabulary on her own.

For practical purposes there are no such things as transferable higher skills of problem solving and reading comprehension. The ability to solve a math problem depends on having a specifically relevant and available math vocabulary. The ability to comprehend a printed text depends on having a specifically relevant and available linguistic vocabulary that comprises at least 90 percent of the words of the text. The vague hope that students will be able to apply what they know in depth about supermarkets to new domains is not sustained by experience or psychological theory.

That is not to say that the mental transfer of structure from one domain to another never occurs. But such analogous thinking is rare. It represents the pinnacle of human thought—the epitome of creative thinking. When it happens, a new art form or field of thought is born. The great physicist Erwin Schroedinger wrote a little book entitled

"What Is Life?" in which he suggested that life is a kind of crystal that enables the life molecule to replicate itself as do the molecules of a crystal. This thought transfer from physics to biology was so captivating that it caused a whole generation of physicists to turn their attention to biology, resulting in the Crick-Watson discovery of DNA, and ultimately in the transformation of modern biology and medicine. For most of us, though, most of the time, such leaps of thought are very rare precisely because they are so difficult.

Our American faith that teaching students biology will teach them "the nature of science," or that teaching students to think critically about the Civil War will teach them how to think critically about current affairs is a misplaced faith that is supported neither by large-scale results nor by the laboratory. The practical result of our faith in the transferability of higher skills has been an incoherent curriculum that is especially damaging to those students who have not gained broad academic knowledge outside of school.

Notes

Preface

1. An excellent short account and up-to-date summary of the research can be found in Daniel T. Willingham, "How Knowledge Helps: It Speeds and Strengthens Reading Comprehension, Learning—and Thinking," *American Educator*, Spring 2006, available online at: http://www.aft.org/pubs-reports/american_educator/issues/spring06/willingham.htm. I have also included an appendix, "Skill Is Content, Content Skill," in which I summarize the findings.

Chapter 1: The Inspiring Idea of the Common School

1. Ruth Miller Elson, *Guardians of Tradition: American Schoolbooks of the Nineteenth Century* (Lincoln: University of Nebraska Press, 1964); J. Merton England, "The Democratic Faith in American Schoolbooks of the Republic, 1783–1861," *American Quarterly* 15 (1963): 191–99. In the early 1890s a typical allocation of classroom time in elementary school was: spelling 16 percent, writing 7 percent, English grammar 10 percent, arithmetic 19 percent, drawing 7 percent, history and geography 16 percent, natural science 6 percent, and music 7 percent. William J. Reese, *America's Public Schools: From the Common School to "No Child Left Behind"* (Baltimore: Johns Hopkins University Press, 2005), 110.
2. See Gordon S. Wood, *The Radicalism of the American Revolution* (New York: Vintage Books, 1993), esp. 102–3.
3. James Madison, *Federalist No. 55*, "The Total Number of the House of Representatives," *New York Packet*, February 15, 1788.

4. Benjamin Rush, "Thoughts upon the Mode of Education Proper in a Republic," from *A Plan for the Establishment of Public Schools and the Diffusion of Knowledge in Pennsylvania* . . . (Philadelphia: Thomas Dobson, 1786), reprinted in *Essays on Education in the Early Republic,* ed. Frederick Rudolph (Cambridge, MA: Harvard University Press, 1965), 9–23.

5. From George Washington's last will and testament: "It has been my ardent wish to see a plan devised on a liberal scale, which would have a tendency to sprd systemactic ideas through all parts of this rising Empire, thereby to do away local attachments and State prejudices, as far as the nature of things would, or indeed ought to admit, from our National Councils." Washington, *The Will,* in *The Papers of George Washington, Retirement Series,* ed. W. W. Abbot, vol. 4: *April–December 1799* (Charlottesville: University Press of Virginia, 1999), 477–492.

6. Andrew S. Draper, "Origin and Development of the New York Common School System," appendix in Sidney Sherwood, *The University of the State of New York: History of Higher Education in the State of New York* (Washington, DC: Government Printing Office, 1900).

7. Carl F. Kaestle, *Pillars of the Republic: Common Schools and American Society, 1780–1860* (New York: Hill and Wang, 1983).

8. Samuel S. Randall, *The Common School System of the State of New York* . . . (Troy, NY: Johnson and Davis, Steam Press Printers, 1851), 58.

9. Randall, *Common School System,* 26, 57.

10. Alexis de Tocqueville, *Democracy in America,* trans. Gerald E. Bevan (London: Penguin, 2003), 355, 356, 364.

11. "The ideas of economists and political philosophers, both when they are right and when they are wrong, are more powerful than is commonly understood. Indeed the world is ruled by little else. Practical men, who believe themselves to be quite exempt from any intellectual influence, are usually the slaves of some defunct economist." J. M. Keynes, *The General Theory of Employment, Interest and Money* (New York: Harcourt Brace, 1936), "Concluding Notes."

12. The most recent data can be found in Mark Bauerlein, *The Dumb-*

est *Generation: How the Digital Age Stupefies Young Americans and Jeopardizes Our Future (Or, Don't Trust Anyone under 30)* (New York: Jeremy P. Tarcher/Penguin, 2008).

13. See the chart on page 88.

14. They were not ignored by the popular press. *Life* ran a feature story on the Florida school, and *Reader's Digest* ran one on the school in the Bronx.

15. The list of schools and much other information can be found at www.coreknowledge.org.

16. An excellent short account and up-to-date summary of the research can be found in Daniel T. Willingham, "How Knowledge Helps: It Speeds and Strengthens Reading Comprehension, Learning—and Thinking," *American Educator,* Spring 2006, available online at: http://www.aft.org/pubs-reports/american_educator/issues/spring06/willingham.htm.

17. The title was "Washing Clothes." See J. D. Bransford and M. K. Johnson, "Contextual Prerequisites for Understanding: Some Investigations of Comprehension and Recall," *Journal of Verbal Learning and Verbal Behavior* 11 (1972): 717–26.

18. "Australia Brought Down to Earth," *Guardian Online,* January 20, 2008.

19. E. D. Hirsch, Jr., *The Knowledge Deficit* (New York: Houghton Mifflin, 2006).

20. See page 110, below.

21. As well as their twentieth-century successors Gramsci, Bagley, and Kandel. See pages 37–38, 63, below.

22. Webster moves from the solar system to the "Geography of the Surface of the Globe, Oceans, Mountains, Rivers, etc."; "Of the Rivers in the United States, Lakes, Falls, etc."; "Of the First Peopling of America, and a Description of the Natives"; "Of the Discovery and Settling of America by Europeans"; "Of the Discovery and Settlement of North America"; "Of Indian Wars"; "Of Political Events"; "Of Military Events"; "Of Bills of Credit"; "Of Piracy in the American Seas"; "Of Diseases and Remarkable Events"; and "Of Controversies and Dissensions among the Colonies."

23. See page 152, below.

24. The Royal Spanish Academy was founded in 1713, and the king of

Spain, Philip V, approved its creation on October 3, 1714. Its purpose was to "fix the words and terms of the Castilian language in their greatest propriety, elegance and purity." Its continually updated dictionary continues to be the basis of school instruction in Spanish.

25. Horace Mann, "12th Annual Report [1848]," in *The Republic and the School,* ed. Lawrence Cremin (New York: Teachers College Press, 1957), 79–112.

26. Joseph J. Ellis, *After the Revolution: Profiles of Early American Culture* (New York: W. W. Norton, 1979), 170.

27. I do not advocate a national curriculum imposed from Washington. See pages XXX–XX, below.

28. Rush, "Thoughts upon the Mode of Education Proper in a Republic."

29. This is the English-language version of the term *Öffentlichkeit* made current by the German philosopher Jürgen Habermas, whose concepts have been influential in recent sociology. Habermas, *Strukturwandel der Öffentlichkeit: Untersuchungen zu einer Kategorie der bürgerlichen Gesellschaft* (Neuwied: Luchterhand, 1962).

30. See Jeff Weintraub and Krishan Kumar, eds., *Public and Private in Thought and Practice: Perspectives on a Grand Dichotomy* (Chicago: University of Chicago Press, 1997).

31. John Rawls, *A Theory of Justice,* rev. ed. (Cambridge, MA: Belknap Press of Harvard University Press, 1999), 462.

32. Kaestle, *Pillars of the Republic.*

33. A key figure is Col. Francis W. Parker, who at the end of the nineteenth and beginning of the twentieth centuries began introducing ideas into his schools from the Romantic tradition of Rousseau, Froebel, and Pestalozzi.

34. A good brief summary of cognitive science on this issue is D. Willingham, "Critical Thinking: Why Is It So Hard to Teach?" *American Educator,* Summer 2007, 9–19.

35. Elson, *Guardians of Tradition.*

36. See Linda Perlstein, *Tested: One American School Struggles to Make the Grade* (New York: H. Holt, 2007).

37. See appendix 2.

38. Christopher Jencks, "What's Behind the Drop in Test Scores?" *Working Papers for a New Society* 6 (July–August 1978): 29–41.

39. See Steve Farkas and Jean Johnson with Ann Duffett and Joanna McHugh, *A Lot to Be Thankful For: What Parents Want Children to Learn about America* (Washington, DC: Public Agenda, 1998). This is the executive summary: "In an age of cynicism, the parents of America still believe in their country—and they want the public schools to teach their children to believe as well. *A Lot to Be Thankful For* focuses on what parents consider the key American values, and to our knowledge is the first to specifically seek out parents who have immigrated here, as well as U.S.-born ones. . . . America's parents have absorbed the principles of the Bill of Rights, even though few of them can fit a particular freedom to a given amendment. They believe in personal freedom, tolerance toward others, and hard work—and they think "bad citizens" include the lazy or intolerant. Finally, parents of all backgrounds firmly believe the schools must teach immigrant children to speak English as quickly as possible, both as a survival skill and as a symbol of their intent to become Americans. They also want schools to teach the common values of American society. Yet this commitment to English and assimilation does not translate into a fear of immigrants themselves. The parents we surveyed fear division, not diversity. And one of the greatest fears voiced by parents is a fear of something that could only happen in their own hearts: they fear taking the United States for granted." See http://www.public agenda.org/specials/thankful/thankful.htm.

40. Jean Johnson and Ann Duffett, *Where We Are Now: Twelve Things You Need to Know about Public Opinion and Public Schools* (Washington, DC: Public Agenda, 2003).

41. See my earlier book *The Schools We Need: And Why We Don't Have Them* (New York: Doubleday, 1996), 71–79. I do not discuss John Dewey in this book. He wrote so much over so long a period, and not always consistently, that debates over Dewey always become fruitless and distracting. To my mind, the most telling critique of Dewey's educational ideas are to be found in the final chapters of Richard Hofstadter, *Anti-Intellectualism in American Life* (New York : Vintage Books, 1963). Hofstadter notes that Dewey's views

depend on a "pre-established harmony" between the natural development of the child and the good of society—a doubtful proposition in Hofstadter's opinion and mine. My term for this point of view is "providentialism," which I discuss in the next chapter. The ideas that count practically for our schools are the maxims and practices of teachers gained from their training in education schools, as I discuss in chapter 2.

42. Reinhold Niebuhr, *Moral Man and Immoral Society: A Study in Ethics and Politics* (New York: Scribner, 1932).

43. These dissenters, chiefly William Bagley, Isaac Kandel, and Antonio Gramsci, are discussed below, pages 37–38, 63.

44. George Counts, "Dare Progressive Education Be Progressive?" *Progressive Education* 9 (April 1932): 260.

45. Probably the best critique of this "pre-established harmony" between concrete activities, individual development, and the needs of society is to be found in Hofstadter, *Anti-Intellectualism in American Life.*

46. Here from the Bank Street School for Children in Manhattan is a typical mission statement: "We seek to strengthen not only individuals, but the community as well, including family, school, and the larger society in which adults and children, in all their diversity, interact and learn. We see in education the opportunity to build a better society." http://www.bnkst.edu/sfc/.

Chapter 2: Sixty Years without a Curriculum

1. Patricia Cohen, "Dumb and Dumber: Are Americans Hostile to Knowledge?" *New York Times,* February 14, 2008.

2. And not just in the United States: here is a statement from Britain, the Hadow Report of 1931: "Applying these considerations to the problem before us, we see that the curriculum is to be thought of in terms of activity and experience rather than of knowledge to be acquired and facts to be stored." See http://www.dg.dial.pipex.com/documents/hadow/3107.shtml. See also http://www.youtube.com/watch?v=opXKmwg8VQM.

3. Diane Ravitch, *Left Back: A Century of Failed School Reforms* (New York: Simon and Schuster, 2000), 171–74, 183–88.

4. Isaac Kandel, "Prejudice the Garden towards Roses," reprinted in Diane Ravitch and Wesley Null, eds., *Forgotten Heroes of American Education: The Great Tradition of Teaching Teachers* (Greenwich, CT: Information Age, 2006), 401–11. Kandel and his friend William Bagley, both professors at Teachers College, were the two most distinguished opponents of the new anti-curriculum movement. They could not have known the as yet-unpublished prison writings by their Italian contemporary Antonio Gramsci, which powerfully supported their view.

5. Herbert M. Kliebard, *The Struggle for the American Curriculum, 1893–1958*, 3rd ed. (New York: Routledge Falmer, 2004).

6. Ravitch, *Left Back*, 296–97.

7. This was Gramsci's point in his criticism of the anti-curriculum movement in his *Notebooks* from the prison where he had been placed by Mussolini. Despite his plain words, anti-curriculum educators have still tried to claim Gramsci because of his impeccable leftist credentials, but very unconvincingly. See H. Giroux, "Rethinking Cultural Politics and Radical Pedagogy in the Work of Antonio Gramsci," *Educational Theory* 49 (1999): 1–19. Gramsci wrote, "Today the tendency is to abolish every kind of 'disinterested' (not immediately interested) and 'formative' school and to leave only a reduced number of them for a tiny elite of ladies and gentlemen who do not have to think of preparing themselves for a professional future, and to spread every more widely the specialized professional schools in which the destiny of the pupil and his future activity are predetermined. The crisis will find a solution which rationally should follow these lines: a single humanistic, formative primary school of general culture which will correctly balance the development of ability for manual (technical, industrial) work with the development of ability for intellectual work. From this type of single school, following repeated tests for professional aptitude, the pupil will pass either into one of the specialized schools or into productive work." This translation is by Louis Marks in Antonio Gramsci, *The Modern Prince and Other Writings* (New York: International Publishers, 1968), 127.

8. Ravitch, *Left Back*, 297ff.

9. See pages 48–55, below.

10. P. Woodring, "The Growth of Teacher Education," in *Teacher Education*, 74th Yearbook of the National Society for the Study of Education, ed. K. Ryan (Chicago: University of Chicago Press, 1975).

11. Geraldine Jonçich Clifford and James W. Guthrie, *Ed School: A Brief for Professional Education* (Chicago: University of Chicago Press, 1988).

12. William Heard Kilpatrick, "The Project Method," *Teachers College Record* 19 (September 1918): 319–34. Through the wonders of YouTube one can actually listen to Kilpatrick lecturing and get the flavor of his pedagogical evangelism: see http://www.youtube.com/watch?v=opXKmwg8VQM.

13. Ravitch, *Left Back*, 240–41.

14. Quoted by Larry Cuban in "The Open Classroom: Schools without Walls Became All the Rage during the Early 1970s: Were They Just Another Fad?" *Education Next* (Spring 2004).

15. See Ravitch, *Left Back;* Lawrence A. Cremin, *The Transformation of the School: Progressivism in American Education, 1876–1957* (New York: Knopf, 1961); and Herbert M. Kliebard, *The Struggle for the American Curriculum, 1893–1958,* 3rd ed. (New York : RoutledgeFalmer, 2004).

16. International Association for the Evaluation of Educational Achievement, *Science Achievement in Seventeen Countries: A Preliminary Report* (Oxford: Pergamon, 1988), 2.

17. Institute of Education Sciences, "Highlights from PISA 2006: Performance of U.S. 15-Year-Old Students in Science and Mathematical Literacy in an International Context," U.S. Department of Education, 2008. http://nces.ed.gov/pubs2008/2008016_1.pdf. For further discussion of our achievement gap with other nations, see pages 123–25, below.

18. Steven Zemelman, Arthur A. Hyde, and Harvey Daniels, *Best Practice: New Standards for Teaching and Learning in America's Schools* (Portsmouth, NH: Heinemann, 1998), 15.

19. Frederic Bartlett, *Remembering* (Cambridge: Cambridge University Press, 1932).

20. Jeanne S. Chall, *The Academic Achievement Challenge: What Really Works in the Classroom?* (New York: Guilford, 2000).

21. Richard Hofstadter, in his discussion of Dewey's educational the-

ories, uses Leibnitz's term "pre-established harmony." Richard Hofstadter, *Anti-Intellectualism in American Life* (New York: Knopf, 1963). See esp. chaps. 13 and 14.

22. As Niebuhr pointed out. He warned the progressives in the 1930s that secular human affairs are not governed by a beneficent and divine human nature but rather by a very defective human nature. This same tragic sense animated Madison and Lincoln. See Reinhold Niebuhr, *Moral Man and Immoral Society* (New York: Scribner, 1932).

23. William Wordsworth, *The Prelude,* 1.14–18.

24. T. E. Hulme, "Romanticism and Classicism," in Hulme, *Speculations: Essays on Humanism and the Philosophy of Art,* ed. Herbert Read (London: Routledge and Paul, 1936), 118.

25. William Wordsworth, "Lines composed a few miles above Tintern Abbey, on Revisiting the Banks of the Wye during a tour, July 13, 1798," ll. 122–23.

26. David Steiner and Susan Rozen, "Preparing Tomorrow's Teachers: An Analysis of Syllabi from a Sample of America's Schools of Education," in *A Qualified Teacher in Every Classroom? Appraising Old Answers and New Ideas,* ed. Frederick M. Hess, Andrew J. Rotherman, and Kate Walsh, 119–48 (Cambridge, MA: Harvard Education Press, 2004). In fairness, I *was* invited to speak once at the Harvard School of Education and once at Teachers College Columbia. But those gestures of openness should be balanced by the hysterical reviews of my books in the *Harvard Educational Review* and *Teachers College Bulletin,* the upshot of which was in every case: "Don't read this awful book." The *Teachers College Bulletin* honored *Cultural Literacy* with two fiercely hostile reviews in one issue, which was, I am told, a first. The review in *TCB* of my most recent book, *The Knowledge Deficit,* calls it an "infomercial" designed to sell my Core Knowledge books. That particular ad hominem "he's just-doing-it-for-the-money" dismissal is the current response in lieu of a counterargument. In fact, I get no money from the Core Knowledge books, having from the start assigned all royalties to the foundation, from which I also receive no money.

27. Alternative names such as "social reconstructionism" get added

according to the tastes of the author. It turns out, though, that all the philosophies are versions of just two—student-centered progressivism, and teacher-centered essentialism. The first is the anti-curriculum, forward-looking, (good) point of view, the second the pro-curriculum, backward-looking, (bad) point of view.

28. Myra Pollack Sadker and David Miller Sadker, *Teachers, Schools, and Society*, 4th ed. (New York: McGraw-Hill, 1997). The web site questionnaire is at: http://highered.mcgraw-hill.com/sites/0072877723/student_view0/chapter9/what_philosophy_is_this_.html.

29. These are omnipresent phrases. Two book-length examples of the ideological polarization are Richard L. Allington, *Big Brother and the National Reading Curriculum: How Ideology Trumped Evidence* (Portsmouth, NH: Heinemann, 2002); and David C. Berliner and Bruce J. Biddle, *The Manufactured Crisis: Myths, Fraud, and the Attack on America's Public Schools* (Reading, MA: Addison-Wesley, 1995).

30. F. Niyi Akinnaso, "The Consequences of Literacy in Pragmatic and Theoretical Perspectives," *Anthropology and Education Quarterly* 12 (Autumn 1981): 163–200.

31. These are, incidentally, among the best-performing schools within the charter-school universe; see http://coreknowledge.org/CK/about/research/index.htm.

32. This is a much-debated issue. Every research report on the performance of charter schools has been followed by complaints from either anticharter or procharter advocates about the methodology of the research and about whether there is a statistically significant difference between the generally poor-performing charter schools and the generally poor-performing regular schools that they were supposed to improve upon. One point is so glaringly obvious from these reports that one hardly needs to delve into them very deeply; the *average* difference in performance between charters and regular schools is not great. For instance, studies conducted by the U.S. Department of Education's Institute of Education Sciences find that regular schools have done slightly better in reading than the charter schools have and, moreover, that this result is "statistically significant." But the difference they found is 0.11 of a stan-

dard deviation, a very small effect size. With a need for a vast improvement in our schools, it is the *magnitude* of the effect that educational reformers need to be looking at rather than studying the entrails of statistical significance.

33. According to Public Agenda, some 82 percent of parents and 80 percent of teachers say that definite curriculum guidelines would be desirable and improve student performance. See http://www .publicagenda.org/issues/major_proposals_detail.cfm?issue_type =education&list=2.

34. Proponents of choice programs point to successes in Europe such as Ireland and Sweden but tend to ignore the implication that these programs work well in conjunction with a common core curriculum.

35. Hanna Skandera and Richard Sousa, *School Figures: The Data behind the Debate* (Stanford, CA: Hoover Institution Press, Stanford University, 2003).

36. Robert A. Fox and Nina K. Buchanan, "School Choice in the Republic of Ireland: An Unqualified Commitment to Parental Choice," National Center for the Study of Privatization in Education, paper # 157, 2008. http://www.ncspe.org/publications_files/ OP157.pdf.

37. One example I know of is the Challenge Foundation, which specializes in supporting charter schools. See the web site: http:// teamcfa.net/. The first aim of the schools it supports is listed as "Commitment to Core Curriculum."

38. Richard D. Kahlenberg, *Tough Liberal: Albert Shanker and the Battles over Schools, Unions, Race, and Democracy* (New York: Columbia University Press, 2007). We universalists would, for example, include disadvantaged white males from Appalachia.

39. Of course, very little could be said about Gramsci's educational views in the 1930s. His prison notebooks were published after World War II.

40. Antonio Gramsci, *Selections from the Prison Notebooks of Antonio Gramsci,* ed. and trans. Quintin Hoare and Geoffrey Nowell Smith (New York: International Publishers, 1971), 24, 40.

41. See http://www.publicagenda.org/issues/major_proposals_detail .cfm?issue_type=education&list=2.

Chapter 3: Transethnic America and the Civic Core

1. Taken from the highly typical pre-2006 Social Studies standards for Arkansas. These have been since revised on the recommendations of a consulting group of which I was a member. See http://arkansased.org/teachers/frameworks2.html#Social.
2. Johann Gottlieb Fichte, *Addresses to the German Nation* (1806), ed. Gregory Moore (New York: Cambridge University Press, 2008).
3. This was the austere political idea of America celebrated by Hannah Arendt in *The Human Condition* (Chicago: Chicago University Press, 1958).
4. "Address before the Young Men's Lyceum, Springfield, Illinois, Jan. 27, 1838," in *The Collected Works of Abraham Lincoln*, vol. 1, ed. Roy P. Basler et al. (New Brunswick, NJ: Rutgers University Press, 1953), 112.
5. Garry Wills, *Lincoln at Gettysburg: The Words That Remade America* (New York: Simon and Schuster, 1992).
6. James Madison, "Memorial and Remonstrance against Religious Assessments," 1785, in *The Papers of James Madison*, vol. 8, ed. Robert Rutland and William Rachal (Chicago: University of Chicago Press, 1973), 298–304.
7. He continues: "In faith and hope the world will disagree, / But all mankind's concern is charity." Alexander Pope, *Essay on Man*, epistle 3, 307ff.
8. "The rights of conscience we never submitted, we could not submit. We are answerable for them to our God. The legitimate powers of government extend to such acts as are injurious to others. But it does me no injury for my neighbour to say there are twenty gods, or no god. It neither picks my pocket nor breaks my leg." Thomas Jefferson, *Notes on the State of Virginia* [1781], ed. Merrill D. Peterson (New York: Library of America, 1984), Query XVII.
9. *Encyclopedia Britannica*, 11th ed., s.v. "Deism."
10. James Madison, *Federalist No. 10*, "The Utility of the Union as a Safeguard against Domestic Faction and Insurrection," *Daily Advertiser*, November 22, 1787.

11. G. K. Chesterton remarked on this moderating and patriotic tenor in the church services he attended on his American visit. G. K. Chesterton, *What I Saw in America* (New York: Dodd, Mead, 1923).

12. Max Lerner, "Constitution and Court as Symbols," *Yale Law Journal* 46 (1937): 1290–319. See also Chesterton, *What I Saw in America*. The Constitution, Chesterton continues, "is founded on a creed. America is the only nation in the world that is founded on creed. That creed is set forth with dogmatic and even theological lucidity in the Declaration of Independence" (7). And further: "The great American experiment; the experiment of a democracy of diverse races which has been compared to a melting-pot. But even that metaphor implies that the pot itself is of a certain shape and a certain substance; a pretty solid substance. The melting-pot must not melt. The original shape was traced on the lines of Jeffersonian democracy; and it will remain in that shape until it becomes shapeless"(8).

13. Samuel S. Randall, *The Common School System of the State of New York . . .* (Troy, NY: Johnson and Davis, Steam Press Printers, 1851), 236.

14. Richard Rorty, "The Priority of Democracy to Philosophy," in Rorty, *Objectivity, Relativism, and Truth: Philosophical Papers,* vol. 1 (Cambridge: Cambridge University Press, 1990). This debate is reflected in divisions on the Supreme Court between original-content interpretations of the Constitution and living-document interpretations.

15. Samuel P. Huntington, *Who Are We? The Challenges to America's National Identity* (New York: Simon and Schuster, 2004). See also Michael Walzer, "What Does It Mean to Be an 'American'?" *Social Research* 71 (Fall 2004): 633–54.

16. This observation by no means diminishes or disputes that the republican ideal of equality and the accountability of leaders to the people evolved out of a specifically British tradition. The claim here is the familiar one that that republican tradition became *generalized* in the United States into a universal cosmopolitan ideal. See Gordon S. Wood, *The Radicalism of the American Revolution* (New York: Knopf, 1992).

17. Salma Hale, *A History of the United States* (1823), and subsequent editions.

18. Herman Melville, *Redburn: His First Voyage* (1849), chap. 33.

19. See, for example, George Washington's letter to the mayor and aldermen of New York City in 1785, when it was the capital of the new "nation." "I pray that Heaven may bestow its choicest blessings on your City. That the devastations of War, in which you found it, may soon be without a trace. That a well regulated and benificial Commerce may enrichen your Citizens. And that, your State (at present the Seat of the Empire) may set such examples of wisdom and liberality, as shall have a tendency to strengthen and give permanency to the Union at home, and credit and respectability to it abroad. The accomplishment whereof is a remaining wish, and the primary object of all my desires." Available at: http:// etext.virginia.edu/etcbin/toccer-new2?id=WasFi28.xml&images= images/modeng&data=/texts/engl. In 1794 Washington made clear by his will that he wished a common education to be the foundation of the "rising empire": "For these reasons, it has long been an ardent wish of mine, to see some plan adopted by which a general and liberal diffucion of learning could be dissiminated, systematically, through all parts of this rising empire; thereby, and as far the nature of the thing will admit and in itself would be proper, to do away local attachments, and State prejudices from our public councels. Hoping that so desireable an object will 'ere long be viewed in the important light I think it merits, my mind is unable to contemplate any measure more likely to effect it than the establishment of a University; where young men from *all parts* of the United States (after having passed through a preparative course of education) may, under Professors of the first reputation in the different branches of literature, Arts and Sciences, compleat their studies; and get fixed in the principles of the Constitution, understand the Laws, and the true interests and policy of their Country, as well as the professions they mean to pursue. And moreover (which is not the least, among the advantages of such a plan) by forming acquintances with each other in early life, avoid those local prejudicies and habitual jealousies which, when carried to excess, are never failing sources of disquietude in the pub-

lic mind, and but two pregnant of mischievous consequences." Available at: http://etext.virginia.edu/etcbin/toccer-new2?id=Was Fi34.xml&images=images/modeng&data=/texts/english/modeng/ parsed&tag=public&part=all.

20. Benjamin Franklin to Peter Collinson, 1753, in *The Writings of Benjamin Franklin,* vol. 2: *Philadelphia, 1726–1757.* Available at: http://www.historycarper.com/resources/twobf2/contents.htm.

21. Valuable discussions can be found in Jeff Weintraub and Krishan Kumar, eds., *Public and Private in Thought and Practice: Perspectives on a Grand Dichotomy* (Chicago: University of Chicago Press, 1997).

22. George Washington to the secretary of state, December 15, 1794, in *The Writings of George Washington,* vol. 34, ed. John C. Fitzpatrick. Available at: http://etext.virginia.edu/toc/modeng/public/ WasFi34.html.

23. Randolph Bourne, "Trans-National America," *Atlantic Monthly,* July 1916, 86–97.

24. Isaiah Berlin, "Two Concepts of Liberty," in Berlin, *Four Essays on Liberty* (London: Oxford University Press, 1969).

25. Lincoln was a proponent of expatriation of blacks to Liberia, but as a political expedient, because of the deep-seatedness of racism among whites, not because he believed it was an absolute necessity. "You and we are different races. We have between us a broader difference than exists between almost any other two races. Whether it is right or wrong I need not discuss, but this physical difference is a great disadvantage to us both, as I think your race suffer very greatly, many of them by living among us, while ours suffer from your presence. In a word we suffer on each side. If this is admitted, it affords a reason at least why we should be separated." "Address on Colonization to a Committee of Colored Men," Washington, D.C. August 14, 1862, in Abraham Lincoln, *Speeches and Writings, 1859–1865,* ed. Don E. Fehrenbacher (New York: Library of America, 1989).

26. Matthew H. Nitecki and Doris V. Nitecki, eds., *Evolutionary Ethics* (Albany: State University New York Press, 1993).

27. Ernest Gellner, *Nations and Nationalism* (Oxford: Blackwell, 1983).

28. Thomas Jefferson, Elementary School Act, 1817, in *The Writings*

of Thomas Jefferson, Memorial Edition, ed. Andrew A. Lipscomb and Albert Ellery Bergh, 20 vols. (Washington, DC: Thomas Jefferson Memorial Association, 1903–4), 17:440.

29. Jefferson to M. Correa de Serra, November 1817, in *Writings of Jefferson,* ed. Lipscomb and Bergh, 15:156.
30. Jefferson to John Adams, October 1813, in *Writings of Jefferson,* ed. Lipscomb and Bergh, 13:396.
31. Benedict Anderson, *Imagined Communities: Reflections on the Origin and Spread of Nationalism,* rev. ed. (New York: Verso, 1991), 145.
32. To be distinguished from the reality of pluralism in American society as traced by Milton Gordon, Nathan Glazer, and other scholars.
33. For a history of twentieth-century schoolbooks in early grades, see Anne-Lise Halvorsen, "The Origins and Rise of Elementary Social Studies, 1884–1941" (PhD diss., University of Michigan, 2006).
34. Halvorsen, "Origins and Rise of Elementary Social Studies."
35. Robert Frost, "After Apple-Picking," in Frost, *North of Boston* (London: D. Nutt, 1914); Hofstadter, *Anti-Intellectualism in American Life* (New York: Vintage Books, 1963).
36. Gordon S. Wood, *Revolutionary Characters: What Made the Founders Different* (New York: Penguin, 2006).
37. G. W. F. Hegel made his initial reputation in *The Phenomenology of Spirit* (1807) with the insight that human ideas and institutions dissolve into their contraries. It is also the theme of a fine poem by William Blake, "The Mental Traveller."
38. See Richard Rorty, "The Unpatriotic Academy," *New York Times,* February 13, 1994, reprinted in Rorty, *Philosophy and Social Hope* (New York: Penguin, 1999).
39. Anderson, *Imagined Communities.* George Orwell makes a similar contrast between nationalism and patriotism in his "Notes on Nationalism," in *The Collected Essays, Journalism, and Letters of George Orwell,* ed. Sonia Orwell and Ian Angus (New York: Harcourt, Brace, Jovanovich, 1968). I was alerted to Orwell's essay by Todd Gitlin in his evocative book *The Intellectuals and the Flag* (New York: Columbia University Press, 2006).
40. Anderson, *Imagined Communities,* 154.

Chapter 4: Linguistic America and the Public Sphere

1. See the final section of this chapter.
2. R. H. Thouless, "Map of Educational Research" (Slough, UK: National Foundation for Educational Research, 1969), 211.
3. "There's a Hole in State Standards, and New Teachers Like Me Are Falling Through," *American Educator*, Spring 2008.
4. Heather MacDonald, "Downward Mobility," *City Journal*, Summer 1994, 10–20.
5. Conference on College Composition and Communication and the National Council of Teachers of English, *Students' Right to Their Own Language;* available at: http://sites.unc.edu/taylor/ccc_old/12/sub/state1.html.
6. Lisa Delpit, *Other People's Children: Cultural Conflict in the Classroom* (New York: New Press, 1996), 3.
7. Gordon S. Wood, *Revolutionary Characters: What Made the Founders Different* (New York: Penguin, 2006), 13–15.
8. Regional or group-associated particularities of *oral* language continue to evolve, of course. An important duty of the schools is to teach the uninitiated how this "code switching" from local to formal conventions of speech occurs.
9. A brand name for boys' and men's underwear. "BVD, founded in 1876 by three gentlemen, Messrs. Bradley, Voorhees and Day, is one of the most famous and historically innovative brands in America": see http://www.bvd.com/.
10. Alexander Pope, *An Essay on Criticism*, ll. 475–81.
11. Pope, *Essay on Criticism*, ll. 482–83.
12. Henry Bradley, *The Making of English* (New York: Macmillan, 1904), 79.
13. "From this one law a man can expect to judge every law properly; and he does not need another law book. Let him plan to judge no man in a way that he himself would not want to be judged by that man, if he pursued judgment against him."
14. See Angus McIntosh, M. L. Samuels, and Michael Benskin, *A Linguistic Atlas of Late Mediaeval English*, 4 vols. (Aberdeen: Aberdeen University Press, 1986–87).

15. See Ernest Gellner, *Nations and Nationalism* (Oxford: Blackwell, 1983), for a penetrating account.

16. A forerunner of course was Latin—the standardized written language of the Church.

17. See http://nces.ed.gov/nationsreportcard/ltt/results2004/nat-reading-scalescore.asp.

18. This shared system of unspoken knowledge and values is of course sustained outside of schooling by what is taught in the home and by nationwide experiences. But these sources of needed knowledge are not equally available to all children; hence my emphasis (and that of the Founders) on the school.

19. Richard M. Nixon and George Schultz, meeting in the Oval Office, March 23, 1971. Available at: http://nixon.archives.gov/forresearchers/find/tapes.

20. William Labov, "Rules for Ritual Insults," in *Studies in Social Interaction,* ed. David Sudnow (New York: Academic Press, 1972), 120–69.

21. See E. D. Hirsch, Jr., *The Knowledge Deficit: Closing the Shocking Education Gap for American Children* (Boston: Houghton Mifflin, 2006).

22. E. D. Hirsch, Jr., *Cultural Literacy: What Every American Needs to Know* (Boston: Houghton Mifflin, 1987).

23. Georgia Kosmoski, Geneva Gay, and Edward L. Vockell, "Cultural Literacy and Academic Achievement," *Journal of Experimental Education* 58 (1990): 265–72. Joseph F. Pentony, "Cultural Literacy: A Concurrent Validation," *Educational and Psychological Measurement* 52 (1992): 967–72. For a summary of research reports, see: http://coreknowledge.org/CK/about/research/index.htm.

24. Harold W. Stevenson and James W. Stigler, *The Learning Gap: Why Our Schools Are Failing and What We Can Learn from Japanese and Chinese Education* (New York: Summit, 1992); Jean-Pierre Jarousse, Alain Mingat, and Marc Richard, "La scolarisation maternelle à deux ans: effets pédagogiques et sociaux," *Éducation et Formations* 31 (1992): 3–9. See also M. Duthoit, "L'enfant et l'école: aspects synthétiques du suivi d'un échantillon de vingt mille élèves des écoles," *Éducation et Formations* 16 (1988): 3–13.

25. The NCTE resolution on grammar is available at: http://www
.ncte.org/about/over/positions/category/gram/107492.htm.

26. From the *Time* archives: "Three days before he made the grammatical welkin ring, Winston Churchill was collecting an honorary
degree at Columbia University. In the very hometown of the American language, he was brash enough to decry the 'undue reliance
upon slang. In its right place slang has its virtues, but let us keep a
tight hold of our own mother tongue. . . .' Then he turned up at
New Haven's Soundscriber Corporation, whose workers had put
in overtime hours to finish two electronic recording machines, for
Churchill's use in dictating his memoirs. In gratitude, Churchill
rolled off a recorded message to the workers: 'This is me, Winston
Churchill, speaking himself to you, and I am so glad to be able to
thank you in this remarkable way.' The eyebrows of newspaper editors, the greatest pedants going, shot up. It was, said the New York
Times stiffly, a 'remarkable sentence.' But college professors,
quickly appealed to, proved as disappointing as Balaam. To a man,
they put their O.K. on Churchill's grammar-defying 'This is me'
(a usage that H. L. Mencken, in *The American Language,* has already admitted to 'conversational respectability, even among
rather careful speakers of English'). Said Yale's Robert D. French:
men like Churchill make the English language. Seconded Prince-
ton's Gordon H. Gerould: idiomatic English is good speech,
prissy English is not. Said Columbia's Raymond M. Weaver: 'A
cheer for Mr. Churchill.'" *Time,* April 1, 1946; http://www.time
.com/time/magazine/article/0,9171,792723,00.html.

Chapter 5: Competence and Equality

1. William R. Johnson and Derek Neal, "Basic Skills and the Black-
White Earnings Gap," in T*he Black-White Test Score Gap,*
ed. Christopher Jencks and Meredith Phillips (Washington,
DC: Brookings Institution Press, 1998).

2. OECD, Programme for International Student Assessment, *The
PISA 2003 Assessment Framework, Mathematics, Reading, and
Problem Solving Skills* (Paris: OECD, 2003), http://www.pisa
.oecd.org/dataoecd/46/14/33694881.pdf.

3. The classic treatment is Larry Cuban, *How Teachers Taught: Constancy and Change in American Classrooms, 1890–1990,* 2nd ed. (New York: Teachers College Press, 1993). Note that Cuban does not take up the subject of *what* teachers taught.

4. An alternative theory is that the wrong side of the anti-curriculum movement won out—the vocationalists and administrative progressives over the true progressives. Cuban, *How Teachers Taught;* David F. Labaree, *The Trouble with Ed Schools* (New Haven and London: Yale University Press, 2004).

5. D. C. Berliner, "Our Impoverished View of Educational Reform," *Teachers College Record* 108 (2006): 949–95.

6. Richard Nisbett, "Race, IQ and Scientism," *The Bell Curve Wars,* ed. Steven Fraser (New York: HarperCollins, 1995), 50–52.

7. Kelly Bedard and Insook Cho, "The Test Score Gap across OECD Countries," Preliminary Draft, Department of Economics, University of California, Santa Barbara; available at: http://client .norc.org/jole/SOLEweb/7207.pdf.

8. Karin Chenoweth, *"It's Being Done": Academic Success in Unexpected Schools* (Harvard Education Press, 2007), 167.

9. Good sources are Jeanne S. Chall, *The Academic Achievement Challenge: What Really Works in the Classroom?* (New York: Guilford, 2000); and the summary articles by D. T. Willingham in *American Educator.*

10. Freddie D. Smith, "The Impact of the Core Knowledge Curriculum, a Comprehensive School Reform Model, on Achievement" (PhD diss., University of Virginia, 2003).

11. Alan D. Baddeley, *Human Memory: Theory and Practice,* rev. ed. (Needham Heights, MA: Allyn and Bacon, 1998).

12. E. D. Hirsch, Jr., and David P. Harrington, "Measuring the Communicative Effectiveness of Prose," in *Writing,* ed. J. Dominic, C. Frederickson, and M. Whiteman (Hillsdale, NJ: Erlbaum, 1981), 189–207.

13. This inference is supported by the slowing down of the gap-reducing trends of the earlier twentieth century. See James P. Smith and Finis R. Welch, *Closing the Gap: Forty Years of Economic Progress for Blacks* (Santa Monica, CA: Rand, 1986).

14. This series contains inspiring introductions explaining the simultaneous need for solidarity and competence. They are a wonder-

ful example of the Webster-Jefferson-Mann tradition of American education, the common school tradition.

15. One might be tempted simply to correlate homogeneity with gap narrowing, but the population of Norway is, for example, more homogeneous than that of Canada yet shows *less* homogeneous school-quality results.

16. Betty Hart and Todd R. Risley, "Meaningful Differences in the Everyday Experience of Young American Children" (Baltimore: P. H. Brookes, 1995).

17. Keith E. Stanovich, "Matthew Effects in Reading: Some Consequences of Individual Differences in the Acquisition of Literacy," *Reading Research Quarterly* 21 (1986): 360–407.

18. George A. Miller, "On Knowing a Word," *Annual Review of Psychology* 50 (1999): 1–19.

19. For convenient summaries, see Richard C. Anderson and William E. Nagy, "Word Meanings," in *Handbook of Reading Research*, vol. 2, ed. Barr et al. (White Plains, NY: Longman, 1991); Miller, "On Knowing a Word"; and William E. Nagy, Richard C. Anderson, and Patricia A. Herman, "Learning Word Meanings from Context during Normal Reading," *American Educational Research Journal* 24 (1987): 237–270.

20. The preceding paragraphs were written by Robert Pondiscio, on the Core Knowledge blog, which I consulted on February 11, 2008, to find a recent example of Core Knowledge school success. I have with his permission simply lifted his report verbatim.

21. See http://www.roxburyprep.org/docs/news.htm.

22. See http://www.roxburyprep.org.

23. Jean-Pierre Jarousse, Alain Mingat, and Marc Richard, "La scolarisation maternelle à deux ans: effets pédagogiques et sociaux," *Éducation et Formations* 31 (1992): 3–9. A translation may be found on the Core Knowledge web site at: http://coreknowledge.org/CK/Preschool/frenchequity.htm.

Chapter 6: Competence and Community

1. William R. Johnson and Derek Neal, "Basic Skills and the Black-White Earnings Gap," in *The Black-White Test Score Gap,* ed.

Christopher Jencks and Meredith Phillips (Washington, DC: Brookings Institution Press, 1998), 480–497.

2. Jill Fitzgerald and Timothy Shanahan, "Reading and Writing Relations and Their Development," *Educational Psychologist* 35 (2000): 39–50.

3. See, e.g., J. I. Brown, V. V. Fishco, and G. Hanna, *Nelson-Denny Reading Test, Technical Report, Forms G and H* (Chicago: Riverside, 1993); and W. H. MacGinitie and R. K. MacGinitie, *Gates-MacGinitie Reading Tests, Third Edition, Technical Report* (Chicago: Riverside, 1989).

4. Linda Perlstein, *Tested: One American School Struggles to Make the Grade* (New York: H. Holt, 2007).

5. Barak Rosenshine and Carla Meister, "Reciprocal Teaching: A Review of the Research," *Review of Educational Research* 64 (1994): 479–530.

6. E. D. Hirsch, Jr., "The Knowledge Connection," *Washington Post*, February 16, 2008, A21.

7. Donna R. Recht and Lauren Leslie, "Effect of Prior Knowledge on Good and Poor Readers' Memory of Text," *Journal of Educational Psychology* 80 (1988): 16–20. See also Cordula Artelt, Ulrich Schiefele, and Wolfgang Schneider, "Predictors of Reading Literacy," *European Journal of Psychology of Education* 16 (2001): 363–83; and Wolfgang Schneider, Joachim Körkel, and Franz E. Weinert, "Domain-Specific Knowledge and Memory Performance: A Comparison of High- and Low-Aptitude Children," *Journal of Educational Psychology* 81 (1989): 306–12. This last-cited article is of particular interest in its implications for gap narrowing and equality of opportunity, since it shows that domain-knowledgeable students of low native ability outperform less knowledgeable students of high native ability.

8. E. D. Hirsch, Jr., "Plugging the Hole in State Standards," *American Educator,* Spring 2008.

9. These topics are not necessarily as disconnected as they seem. They happen to be part of the thematically integrated Core Knowledge curriculum. Their scattered character in this example is a good illustration of how difficult it is to do anything coherent in the way of curriculum-based tests without having a specific core curriculum!

10. This is in fact what happens in schools that follow the Core Knowledge curriculum. See Freddie D. Smith, "The Impact of the Core Knowledge Curriculum, a Comprehensive School Reform Model, on Achievement" (PhD diss., University of Virginia, 2003).

11. National Commission on Excellence in Education, *A Nation at Risk: The Imperative for Educational Reform* (Washington, DC: U.S. Department of Education, 1983), 72.

12. *Nation at Risk,* 55.

13. See pages 123–25, above.

14. I summarize the scientific consensus on this score in a technical appendix at the back of this book entitled "Content Is Skill, Skill Content."

15. Stanislas Dehaene, *The Number Sense: How the Mind Creates Mathematics* (New York: Oxford University Press, 1997).

16. K. Anders Ericsson, Neil Charness, Paul J. Feltovich, and Robert R. Hoffman, *The Cambridge Handbook of Expertise and Expert Performance* (New York: Cambridge University Press, 2006).

17. Other, more technical attributes are that the early core must be highly specific, and it must be outlined grade by grade. Without specificity there can be no commonality, and we fall into the vagueness trap of current state standards. Grade-by-grade definiteness is needed because the school year is the key time unit for the student, who usually moves to a new teacher at a new grade level.

18. *Core Knowledge Sequence: Content Guidelines for Grades K-8* (Charlottesville, VA: Core Knowledge Foundation, 1999).

19. Over the years, we have made further adjustments based on experiences of Core Knowledge schools.

20. Eric Hobsbawm and Terence Ranger, eds., *The Invention of Tradition* (Cambridge: Cambridge University Press, 1983).

21. A good alternative example with excellent results is the Roxbury Preparatory Charter School, a public school that serves grades six through eight. The school has developed a highly specific, grade-by-grade curriculum based on an analysis of the Massachusetts state standards (among the best in the country) and of the kinds of knowledge probed by the state tests. The school's web site explains: "Though not every Roxbury Prep standard corresponds directly with the Massachusetts state standards, every Massachu-

setts standard is addressed and receives significant attention in the Roxbury Prep curriculum. Using Roxbury Prep's Curriculum Alignment Template (CAT), teachers ensure that every Massachusetts and Roxbury Prep standard is addressed with a class lesson and that every class lesson addresses at least one standard. Roxbury Prep teachers distribute the academic standards and weekly syllabi to students and families. Syllabi include daily objectives, activities, and homework assignments" (http://www.roxburyprep .org/docs/curriculum.htm). It is a tremendous credit to this school that it has undertaken the immense labor to create this curriculum.

22. According to another mass e-mail, merely listing such examples is totally unacceptable if we are to avoid becoming a totalitarian nation of drones: "Please vote in favor of knowledge creation, not knowledge acquisition. Please vote against Chairman McLeroy's amendment for educational regression! . . . As a Returned Peace Corps Volunteer from the former Soviet Republic of Moldova, I saw first hand what the effects of routine memorization did to an entire population. It produced a generation of people who have difficulty knowing how to think, question or create. Many of the difficulties that they face today stem largely from what the Soviet System turned their schools into. One of my tasks, as a volunteer and teacher there, was to (with the support of the Soros Foundation) bring back critical thinking skills to the people in the former USSR. Never did I think that I would be concerned about these same things in the United States! I am seeing the same types of things happen to the next generation of children in Texas."

23. Sandra Shoiock Roff, Anthony M. Cucchiara, and Barbara J. Dunlap, *From the Free Academy to CUNY: Illustrating Public Higher Education in New York City, 1847–1997* (New York : Fordham University Press, 2000), 4; Thomas Jefferson, Elementary School Act, 1817, in *The Writings of Thomas Jefferson, Memorial Edition,* ed. Andrew A. Lipscomb and Albert Ellery Bergh, 20 vols. (Washington, DC: Thomas Jefferson Memorial Association, 1903–4), 17: 440.

24. Diane Ravitch to author, personal e-mail, March 9, 2008.

25. See http://www.youtube.com/watch?v=opXKmwg8VQM.

26. "It occurred after the thing, therefore because of the thing."

27. Carl F. Kaestle et al., *Literacy in the United States: Readers and Reading since 1880* (New Haven and London: Yale University Press, 1991).

28. See *Westend Journal,* September 28, 2007: "On the front of the building are Melancthon, Asham, Loyola, Thomas Arnold, Horace Mann, Frederick Froebel, Herbart, Pestalozzi, Comenius. Around the corner on the left, over what was and is still labeled its High School, are Dante, Vergil, Aristotle, Plato, Homer, and around the other corner, over what was and is still labeled its Elementary School, are Columbus, Washington, Hamilton, Lincoln and Webster." http://www.westendejournal.com/index.php?news_id=250&issue=27 For a standard listing, see Donald G. Barker, "A Hierarchical Grouping of Great Educators," *Southern Journal of Educational Research* 11 (1977): 23–30. The author's abstract: "Great educators of history were categorized on the basis of their: aims of education, fundamental ideas, and educational theories. They were classed by Ward's method of hierarchical analysis into six groupings: Socrates, Ausonius, Jerome, Abelard; Quintilian, Origen, Melanchthon, Ascham, Loyola; Alciun, Comenius; Vittorino, Basedow, Pestalozzi, Froebel, Montessori; De la Salle, Francke; and Mulcaster, Herbart, Seguin, Binet."

Acknowledgments

As the endnotes make clear, one cannot undertake an overview of American education without incurring massive intellectual debts from philosophers, historians, and cognitive scientists. But endnotes cannot begin to acknowledge how much this book has benefited from the advice of friends, family, and colleagues, many of whom have read and commented on various stages of the manuscript, especially Paul Beston, Linda Bevilaqua, John Bryan, Margaret Chrisman, John Hirsch, Polly Hirsch, Ted Hirsch, Krishan Kumar, Gloria Loomis, Robert Pondiscio, Bob Reid, Becky Thomas, and Dan Willingham. William Frucht of Yale University Press edited the book with an unmatched expertness and intelligence. I am deeply grateful to them all.

Index